Dawn of Behavioural Finance, 1688

Dawn of Behavioural Finance, 1688

By

Vasileios Kallinterakis

Cambridge
Scholars
Publishing

Dawn of Behavioural Finance, 1688

By Vasileios Kallinterakis

This book first published 2024

Cambridge Scholars Publishing

Lady Stephenson Library, Newcastle upon Tyne, NE6 2PA, UK

British Library Cataloguing in Publication Data
A catalogue record for this book is available from the British Library

ISBN: 978-1-0364-1340-8
ISBN (Ebook): 978-1-0364-1341-5

To my beloved Parents, who taught me to think for myself

TABLE OF CONTENTS

LIST OF ILLUSTRATIONS

PREFACE

Behavioural finance was born during the 1980s as the result of a cross-fertilisation between finance and (primarily) psychology, with other disciplines (including sociology and decision science) also contributing to its foundations. The role of psychology in financial decisions was largely downplayed during much of the 20th century, with finance scholars mainly relying on the neoclassical paradigm; drawing on the concept of the Economic Man, this paradigm involved a more mathematical representation of decision-making, aiming at calibrating financial reality via quantitative models. To the extent that this paradigm ignored the human nature of economic agents, it gradually began to be challenged since the 1950s (when Herbert Simon proposed the notion of bounded rationality) and, more so, since the 1970s (when Daniel Kahneman and Amos Tversky denoted the role of prospect theory and biases/heuristics in decision-making). From then on, the trajectory of behavioural finance is, more or less, known; initially challenging market efficiency (a cornerstone of neoclassical finance research), researchers began exploring deviations from efficient pricing (in the form e.g., of return anomalies and predictability), before availing themselves of datasets of more depth (such as e.g., higher frequency data and transaction data/portfolio holdings of retail/institutional investors) to examine various behavioural trading patterns (e.g., herding, disposition effect etc.).

Although the above description of the evolution of behavioural finance is largely accurate, it suggests that the role of psychology in financial decisions was only appreciated in the postwar decades–something not accurate. Evidence from prewar scholarship suggests that the role of psychology in economics, in general, was raised in a series of treatises going as far back as the 18th century; key names in economics, such as Adam Smith, Thorsten Veblen and Jeremy Bentham touched upon behavioural issues in economic life (Camerer et al., 2004; Zak, 2004; Sapra and Zak, 2008), while such issues were even raised by authors of literature aimed at non-academic audiences (Mackay, 1841; Selden, 1919; Clason, 1926). However, it is important to note that none of those authors essentially came close enough to the spirit of modern-day behavioural finance; this was accomplished in the Netherlands long before their time, when Amsterdam hosted the world's first-ever organised stock exchange.

In the year 1688, the Sephardi merchant Joseph de la Vega published a book aiming at describing aspects of the investment life in the then-nascent Dutch stock market. Titled *Confusion of Confusions*, the book analysed technical aspects of trading operations, besides offering a discussion of various forms of investors' behaviour. What is astounding–as shall be depicted in ample detail later on in this book–is that the issues Vega discussed and the behavioural phenomena he described, correspond to concepts systemised by behavioural finance research over three centuries after his time. *Confusion of Confusions* is often cited as (and, indeed, is) the first book ever written on stock market trading and investors' behaviour. However, although it has motivated some academic attention in terms of the trading practices/tools it describes[1], very little discourse exists as regards its importance to behavioural finance, with the book's actual relevance to behavioural finance being extremely under-researched to date.[2]

The book at hand aims at remedying this situation, by conducting a comprehensive study of *Confusion of Confusions* from the perspective of the behavioural finance paradigm. Its crux lies on critically assessing the behavioural trading beliefs/patterns described by Vega in terms of modern behavioural finance theory. To offer some context, this book first embarks on a critical introduction to behavioural finance and how it challenges the neoclassical finance paradigm (Chapter 1). Chapter 2 provides a detailed analysis of *Confusion of Confusions*' historical context, in terms of the author, his Sephardi community and its role in the Dutch maritime trade, the establishment of the Dutch East Indies Company and how this ultimately motivated the launch of the Amsterdam Stock Exchange. The assessment of *Confusion of Confusions* based on the behavioural finance paradigm takes place in Chapter 3, drawing on ample comparisons between issues surfacing in Vega's descriptions/discussions and contemporary behavioural finance concepts. Chapter 4 outlines a series of implications of this study for various stakeholders (researchers; investment community; regulators and policymakers; the Sephardi community).

The book ultimately shows that there is nothing new under the sun; biases, heuristics, and collective behavioural phenomena extensively investigated by behavioural finance scholars were pretty much present in

[1] Examples of such studies include De Marchi and Harrison (1994), Muprhy (1997) and Szpiro (2011).

[2] The only work that has discussed *Confusion of Confusions* from a strictly behavioural finance perspective (albeit with narrow a scope, drawing on a limited number of quotes from it) was the paper by Corzo et al. (2014); a short discussion on the relevance of Vega's book to behavioural finance is also included in Economou et al. (2023).

the 17th century Dutch market. This is rather disturbing, considering that, despite our institutional and technological evolution, we commit errors of judgement remarkably similar to those of investors almost three-and-a-half centuries ago. This clearly shows that, whereas our material civilisation has evolved, the same cannot be argued about our nature; whether we fail or refuse to learn, we still make the same mistakes. *Confusion of Confusions* leaves no doubt about this, thus allowing us to concur that it constitutes the precursor to modern-day behavioural finance.

This further helps elevate Vega's position in behavioural finance scholarship and history; beyond simply treating the writing of *Confusion of Confusions* as simply a pastime for him (which it may also have been)[3], it is shown that its relevance to behavioural finance is far deeper than popularly acknowledged. Whereas his book has often been treated as a literary narrative of his time, it is clear that it contains very precise allusions to concepts that behavioural finance researchers have been working on during the past at least three to four decades. Far from forming a simple popular finance writing (as has often been dubbed), a detailed examination of it reveals that it forms the first actual treatise on behavioural finance issues by way of narration (in his own very unique style, which shall be elaborated on in Chapter 2). To that end, Vega deserves to be treated as the earliest founder of behavioural finance-on whom contemporary researchers can draw for inspiration. Furthermore, this should also suffice to secure him a position within the broad circle of his Sephardi community's scholars who helped shape scientific discourse in several branches of economics and finance during the Renaissance era and its aftermath. The present book helps raise awareness of an aspect of Vega's contribution to scholarship largely underexplored–if not outright downplayed, to date. It is my hope that the reader enjoys it and that it endows him with the motivation to learn more about behavioural finance–which Joseph de la Vega (unknowingly) helped found.

Durham, June 16th, 2024

[3] See Kellenbenz's comments in De la Vega (1957, xi).

ACKNOWLEDGEMENTS

This book was originally motivated via a series of online lectures on *Confusion of Confusions* I delivered in the Spring semester of academic years 2021-22 and 2023-24 for the Continuing Education Department of the University of Liverpool. I would like to thank Dr Glenn Godenho, Academic Director of Continuing Education for the University of Liverpool, for embracing these lectures (as well as any other lectures I have offered to deliver for his department since 2019); I would also like to thank the Department's members of the student support team for their invaluable assistance over the years. Special thanks also go to the participants of those lectures for the support, questions, and comments; ultimately, they helped me realise that expanding on the subject in the form of a book was the right thing to do.

CHAPTER 1

BEHAVIOURAL FINANCE: AN INTRODUCTION

The role of psychology in financial decision-making had been long acknowledged by early classical economists (e.g., A. Smith; W.S. Jevons), who nevertheless harboured reservations as per whether the impact of behavioural/emotional factors could ever be satisfactorily captured in standard economic models (Camerer et al., 2004; Zak, 2004; Sapra and Zak, 2008). This gradually began to change following the evolution of cognitive psychology and decision science, which allowed researchers by the 1980s to develop tools and measures of investors' behaviour. To better understand how Vega's book constitutes the earliest treatise on behavioural finance concepts, this chapter will discuss how behavioural finance evolved as a response to the previously established neoclassical finance paradigm and outline its key principles.

1.1 Neoclassical finance

1.1.1 The Economic Man

The neoclassical (also, known as rational) finance paradigm views financial decision-making largely as a process carried out with (some) mathematical precision, based on quantitative models/formulae. The archetypal representative agent of human behaviour in this paradigm's context is the "Economic Man" (*homo economicus*); first coined as a term by John Stuart Mill in 1836, it entailed two key features, namely rationality and utility-maximisation.[4]

The notion of rationality encompasses several aspects, which will now be presented in some detail. To begin with, rationality initially presupposes investors having complete knowledge and understanding of all information relevant to their decisions. In other words, they know all factors comprising

---

[4] For more on the genealogy of the term, see Bee and Desmarais-Tremblay (2023).

the true model of (i.e., the one that most accurately describes) an economic variable, possessing structural knowledge of the latter. Examples of such knowledge include knowledge about demand/supply functions of that variable, knowledge of how to estimate present and future general equilibrium prices for that variable, as well as knowledge about its stochastic properties over time (Brav and Heaton, 2002). In this context, if an investor, for example, aims at valuing (or forecasting the price of) a stock, the information she has on the factors affecting its price is sufficiently complete to allow her to build the correct valuation/forecasting model. For this to be possible, however, "sufficiently complete" information is not enough.

Enter here the second element of rationality: investors are assumed to be completely rational information processors, who make optimal statistical decisions with zero distortions. Assuming the above holds, investors would then be expected to combine all relevant information the right way to come up with an accurate valuation of an asset (or forecast of its value). This means that they: i) know all relevant information; ii) interpret it correctly; and iii) combine it correctly. Up to this point, the investor is said to bear *consistent beliefs*, which means that the subjective distribution she uses to value a variable (or forecast its future values) is the actual distribution reigning that variable's price-formation process (Sargent, 1993). The next logical step is for the investor to put together an empirical specification (i.e., a model) to capture the formation of the variable's prices (or to generate forecasts of its future values); to ensure the model is the correct one, she needs to enter any relevant factor in that model with the appropriate weight and ensure the model's functional form is correct.[5] In view of the above, this model will then be the true/correct one, whose coefficients can be estimated with no biases (Friedman, 1979) and allow her to reach the correct valuation/forecast for her variable of interest.

An issue arising from the above is whether investor's rationality implies that her expectations are also rational; after all, even the most rational investor with strong and unbiased processing capacity may encounter limitations in her valuations/forecasts, if the information available is bounded. Brav and Heaton (2002) outline this issue as one of information-exploitation versus information-availability. Assuming the rational investor resides in a rational expectations world, she is capable of exploiting the complete set of relevant information perfectly rationally. If the investor, however, resides in a non-rational expectations world, she will be unable to possess knowledge of the complete set of relevant information; in that case,

[5] E.g., whether the model is linear/non-linear, whether the factors entering it are scaled, standardised, in logarithmic form etc., to mention but a few.

she will have to resign herself to applying her rationality to the processing of only the subset of information available to her.[6]

Further aspects of rationality include Bayesian updating and superior foresight (Barberis and Thaler, 2003). The former suggests that investors update their beliefs with any newly incoming information–assuming that the processing of any new information signal is free from distortion. Superior foresight does not mean that the investor's valuations/forecasts are 100% accurate. Errors are not precluded; however, they are treated as a reflection of a lack of performance (i.e., they are due to fatigue or not enough effort)[7] and are assumed not to repeat themselves.

The second feature of the Economic Man is utility-maximisation; according to this, investors compare investment options and choose the one that allows them to enjoy the maximum expected utility. To generate the latter, investors identify each option's possible outcomes and the probability of each outcome's occurrence, before calculating the weighted average of all possible outcomes. In response to the argument that an investor can/need not know the exact probability of each outcome, Savage (1964) proposed the subjective expected utility (SEU) theory, according to which, each investor calculates his own subjective probabilities. Even if she knows that these probabilities entail a higher level of ambiguity, her decisions are presumed not to be affected, since she is assumed to possess consistent beliefs (in which case, her subjective probabilities are presumed to approximate the actual ones).[8] Expected utility theory further predicts that investors are risk-averse, with utility increasing with wealth at a decreasing rate; beyond a certain wealth-threshold, larger amounts of wealth are associated with greater risk. As a result, a risk-averse individual will only accept a risky gamble, if its expected utility exceeds the utility one derives

---

[6] Such conditions would imply structural uncertainty and, in their presence, the investor will be unable to infer the true distribution of their variable of interest and would likely have to learn it from the available data (or experience). See Brav and Heaton (2002) for more on this.

[7] In this case, the possibility of errors being due to lack of full understanding of information processing (which would render them "competence errors" and imply irrationality) is precluded; no recourse also exists to limitations in the computational abilities of the individual, despite the complexity surrounding algorithmic optimisation. For more on the distinction between performance and competence errors, see Stein (1996).

[8] Although it is hard to fathom the subjective probabilities of each individual to satisfy this, the mere identification of those probabilities allows, technically, for the calculation of expected utility; this suggests that, in the context of SEU it is the probabilities of outcomes that influence choices, not our level of confidence in those probabilities.

from a riskless gamble–i.e., as long as gambling makes sense on a risk-adjusted basis.

Expected utility theory relies on the axioms proposed by von Neumann and Morgenstern (1944), which include the properties of completeness, transitivity, independence, continuity, cancellation, dominance and invariance (see the discussion in Tversky and Kahneman, 1986). Completeness refers to the case whereby an individual's available preference options are all comparable; transitivity denotes that choices are consistent[9]; independence suggests that, when comparing two alternatives, we base our choice on their distinct, not common, aspects[10]; continuity implies that no option is infinitely more/less desirable than any other option[11]; cancellation denotes that, if two options yield similar outcomes when a state holds (but not when it does not hold), then that state can be ignored when comparing the two options; dominance is the condition whereby, if option A is better than other options in one state and at least as good in all other states, then A constitutes the dominant option; finally, invariance is about different representations of the same choice problem yielding the same preference (i.e., framing should/does not matter).

As a result, the Economic Man was assumed to be of unbounded cognitive capabilities:[12] he has access to all relevant information, which he can process unbiasedly and which he uses to update his beliefs in a Bayesian fashion. Even when his forecasts are mistaken, his mistakes are not systematic (they are not repeated twice), nor do they confer any emotional impact over him. Being in possession of unbounded cognitive capacity, he is able to handle large computational tasks; this allows him to be familiar with the expected utility of each risky option (since he is aware of all its

---

[9] This condition implies that each option's value is evaluated individually and does not depend on alternative options. Assume the utility of option A is greater than that of B, and B's greater than C's; in this case, you choose A over B, B over C, and A over C. If, for some reason, option C possesses features that render its rejection regrettable for you, then factoring regret into the consequences of choosing option A or B versus C will distort the transitivity principle. In this case, the choice will not be strictly based upon a common measure (utility) but also depend on non-utility related features (regret).

[10] E.g. if you have three options, let A, B and C, and A + C is preferred over B + C, then A will be preferred over B, irrespective of whether one accounts for C or not.

[11] If e.g. option A is preferred over B, and option B is preferred over C, it is possible that there exists a combination A + C viewed by the individual as indifferent to B.

[12] This has been eloquently outlined by Thaler and Sunstein (2009, 7) as follows: "If you look at economics textbooks, you will learn that homo economicus can think like Albert Einstein, store as much memory as IBM's Big Blue, and exercise the willpower of Mahatma Gandhi."

possible outcomes and each outcome's probability) and, to that end, chooses among different options with the aim of maximising his utility.

1.1.2 Market efficiency: Assumptions and criticisms

If the Economic Man dominates capital markets, it is reasonable to assume that traded assets will be priced largely in line with their intrinsic value[13], the latter varying with the flow of information arriving at the market. This market setting is formally deemed to be efficient, in line with Fama et al. (1969) and Fama (1970), who posited that efficient markets are those in which prices respond instantly to any new information and incorporate all available information at any point in time over time.[14] As per this definition, once information is incorporated into prices, it is impossible to realise abnormal returns by trading on this information; the notion here is that, once information arrives, its impact over prices alters the market and creates a new market valuation (different from the one prior to the arrival of the information in the past and also different from the one to arise once new information arrives in the future). As a result, since prices respond instantly to new information and the arrival-rate of new information obeys no specific pattern (i.e., news arrives randomly), the market cannot produce consistent/predictable patterns of prices (Farmer, 2002).[15] Taking together the randomness of news' arrival with the fact that prices respond instantly to news, suggests that, in an efficient market, prices follow a random walk in their formation process.[16]

---

[13] A stock's intrinsic ("fundamental") value is calculated by discounting the sum of the expected cash flows from the stock (e.g. its future dividends, earnings etc.) to the present at a given rate.

[14] The earliest known writings on the role of information in shaping prices can be identified with James Maitland and Yamagata Bantō; see the discussion in Takatsuki and Hisamatsu (2023).

[15] Two things are important to note here: first, even if a pattern were to arise, it would be quickly exploited by investors (or arbitraged away)–and eventually disappear (Farmer, 2002); second, the presence of transaction costs would further contribute to the dissipation of the profitability of any such pattern (Jensen, 1978).

[16] The concept of "random walk" in stock prices was first described by Jules Regnault in 1863 (Jovanovic and Le Gall, 2018); as Gujarati (2003) eloquently described it: "The term random walk is often compared with a drunkard's walk. Leaving a bar, the drunkard moves a random distance *ut* at time *t*, and, continuing to walk indefinitely, will eventually drift farther and farther away from the bar. The same is said about stock prices. Today's stock price is equal to yesterday's stock price plus a random shock." (Gujarati, 2003, 798). For a discussion of early evidence on the random walk, see Woo et al. (2020).

Although, as mentioned above, this means that one cannot beat (i.e., outperform) the market systematically, this does not mean that this can never happen. It is possible, for example, that an asset is temporarily over/underpriced (in which case, you can profit from exploiting its mispricing) or that an asset is riskier than the market average (in which case, by assuming higher risk when trading on it, you can realise an above-market return). As a result, you are rewarded with a return proportionate to the risk you take ("no free lunch").[17]

Contingent on the type of information incorporated in securities' prices, market efficiency can assume three forms (Fama, 1991). A market is weak-form efficient when prices fully reflect all information contained in past price movements. If this holds, then looking at past prices (or past trading data, in general, including for example past volume, turnover etc.) is assumed to contain no relevant information about future prices, thus rendering any attempt at extrapolating from historical prices[18] an exercise in futility.[19] A market is semi-strong form efficient, if prices fully reflect both all relevant publicly available information and all information contained in past price movements (thus suggesting that a market cannot be semi-strong form efficient without being weak-form efficient). In this case, the instant incorporation of new information into prices suggests that any attempt by investors/analysts to compute a stock's fundamental value following the arrival of news will lag behind the market's reaction to the

[17] In reality, "no free lunch" need not coexist with fundamentals-based prices; as Barberis and Thaler (2003) stated, "While both are true in an efficient market, "no free lunch" can also be true in an inefficient market: just because prices are away from fundamental value does not necessarily mean that there are any excess risk-adjusted average returns for the taking" (Barberis and Thaler, 2003, 1057).

[18] The practice of extrapolating from historical prices is more formally known as feedback trading and can entail a host of trading strategies (momentum; contrarian; technical analysis) and practices/tools (stop-loss orders; take-profit orders; portfolio insurance). For a detailed discussion of the literature on feedback trading, see Economou et al. (2023).

[19] Neoclassical finance traditionally tended to view trading on historical prices with ambivalence. Lo et al. (2000, 1705) mention that "It has been argued that the difference between fundamental analysis and technical analysis is not unlike the difference between astronomy and astrology. Among some circles, technical analysis is known as "voodoo finance." And in his influential book A *Random Walk down Wall* Street, Burton Malkiel (1996) concludes that "[u]nder scientific scrutiny, chart-reading must share a pedestal with alchemy."". Nevertheless, there exists a host of evidence (see Hoffmann and Shefrin, 2014 and the discussion therein) suggesting the wide popularity of technical trading strategies among investors.

news–in turn, casting doubt on the usefulness of fundamentals' analysis.[20] Finally, a market is deemed strong-form efficient, if prices reflect all privately held information, all relevant publicly available information and all information contained in past price movements.

Market efficiency presupposes that the trading process is dominated by rational investors who compete against each other using their information to predict securities' future prices (Fama, 1965). Given their competition, securities' prices will, at any point in time, reflect their information and tend to hover around their actual (intrinsic) values. Of course, to the extent that a company's intrinsic value depends upon its earnings' potential (and given that future earnings are impossible to know with certainty), the intrinsic value will always entail an element of uncertainty (Black, 1986); as a result, the actual price will always be an estimate of (and wandering randomly about) the intrinsic value.

In the context of the efficient market hypothesis, it is further possible that some investors do not subscribe to the paradigm of the Economic Man, or indeed any of its features; these investors are deemed irrational and can be accommodated in the neoclassical finance paradigm in two ways. First, even if they are of good size, their trades are assumed to be random (some may under- and others overvalue a stock; some may under- and others overreact to information) and thus, cancel each other out (Fama, 1998). Second, if their trades are correlated (i.e., there exists systematic irrationality) and motivate mispricing, rational investors can eliminate the latter via arbitrage (Friedman, 1953; Fama, 1965).[21] As a result, although

---

[20] The following quote from Mathiopoulos (1994) summarises this eloquently: "Based on the theory of efficient markets, namely that the price of a stock in the market reflects all available information relevant to the course of the underlying corporation, it is worth wondering whether it is the analyst that comes up with the forecast or the stock itself–and which purpose the analyst serves in the end" (author's translation from the Greek original).

[21] Arbitrageurs are investors who earn riskless profits at no cost. As per Hirshleifer (2014, 6): "Arbitrage is the purchase or sale of goods to profit from differences in effective prices across trading venues. The term is used broadly to refer to the exploitation of profit opportunities whenever some assets are overpriced relative to others, based on the idea that buying cheap assets and selling similar but expensive ones can yield a relatively low-risk return." In this case, investors go long on cheap and short on expensive similar assets. Going short implies short selling, namely selling something you do not currently own with the obligation of buying it back at a given price in the future. You obviously do that if you expect the price to fall, the expectation being that overpriced stocks will see their prices fall and underpriced ones their prices rise. The practice of short selling can be traced virtually since the birth of capital markets, as De la Vega (1957) documents (and as shall be discussed

market efficiency does not refute the possibility of non-rational/less-than-perfectly rational investors, it views their impact over the price-formation process to be of no import.[22]

An intriguing view on this issue was advanced by Friedman (1953), who argued that in an efficient market, investors act "as if" they are trying to rationally maximise expected returns with full knowledge of necessary data. "As if" means that the behaviour of individual investors matters little; rather, it is the aggregate outcome of their actions that will have to be rational for the market to be efficient. The presence of "as if" in the efficient markets' paradigm may bring the latter closer to reality (after all, it is hard to presume homogeneity among investors, much less homogeneity in their rationality), yet also complicates things, as it implies that valuing a stock can be an uncertain and extremely vexing process (as it assumes the interaction of traders of various rationality levels). With "as if" the focus now shifts from procedural rationality (which examines whether the strategies and rules underlying behaviour are rational or not) to theoretical rationality (which judges behaviour only by its outcomes, regardless how they were achieved). In this case, an individual reaching a rational decision by chance or imitation (e.g., of his rational peers) is also perceived as

---

later on in this book); for more on this, see also Marco and Van Malle-Sabouret (2007) for arbitrage on the bonds issued by the Dutch East India Company and Dempster et al. (2000) and Bell et al. (2016) for evidence from the 18th century London and Amsterdam markets. Beyond the finance-related literature, very early references to situations reflective of differential pricing of similar items are included in ben Maimon's Ma'aser Sheni 4:21 ("When a person transports produce from a place where it is expensive to a place where it is inexpensive, he should redeem it according to its value in the place he is redeeming it.") from the 2nd-3rd centuries AD; and Wu Ch'eng-en (1973, 304)'s 16th century Chinese novel "Monkey" ("[…] and he told his servants to saddle six horses, but not to let Tripitaka's horse be saddled for the present. Then they all rode down to the river to look. It was true enough that people were walking across the ice. "Where are they going?", asked Tripitaka. "They are traders", said Mr Ch'en, "from the country on the other side of the river. Things that here are worth a hundred strings of cash are worth ten thousand on the other side. And things that are there worth only a hundred are here worth two thousand. So great are the profits to be made that they are willing to undertake the journey even at the risk of their lives.").

[22] Rational or not, investors may well exhibit disagreement as per their interpretation of information due to behavioural factors (biases/heuristics; see next section) as well as persistent differences in opinions (Carlin et al., 2014). The potential of investors' disagreement was not viewed by Fama (1970) as evidence against efficiency "…unless there are investors who can consistently make better evaluations of available information than are implicit in market prices" (Fama, 1970, 388).

rational, thus rendering possession of the formal properties of rationality less important in the attainment of rational outcomes.[23]

Despite early empirical support for market efficiency (Fama, 1965; Fama and Blume, 1966; Ball and Brown, 1968; Jensen, 1968; Fama et al., 1969; Waud, 1970; Scholes, 1972; Keown and Pinkerton, 1981), criticism began to mount shortly thereafter. To begin with, although the neoclassical finance paradigm prided itself over the mathematical calibration of its empirical designs, there exists to date no singular "correct"/"right"/"true" model of asset pricing. This is an issue most prominently reflected in the so-called joint-hypothesis problem (Fama, 1970; 1991); according to this, it is not possible to *ad hoc* test for market efficiency in isolation without considering an asset pricing model. Since, by definition, prices in an efficient market properly incorporate all information, an asset pricing model is needed to quantify how "proper" this incorporation is. As a result, if an anomaly (i.e., a deviation from efficiency) surfaces in the return-generation process, it is hard to assert whether this is due to the market being inefficient or whether this is due to the asset pricing model used being the wrong one. The problem is further aggravated by the established (Cochrane, 2011) "factor zoo", since the huge number (in the hundreds) of common risk factors[24] proposed during the past few decades clearly suggests that it is practically impossible to come up with a single model that works equally well across all markets, time periods and economic conditions/market states. Lo and MacKinlay (1999) further argued that market efficiency needs more hypotheses (related to investors' preferences, information structure, and business conditions) to be added when testing for it. If this were to happen, they argued, that would render testing for market efficiency a test of multiple hypotheses simultaneously, in which case a rejection of

---

[23] See the discussion in Merkle (2007) for more on the issue of theoretical-versus-procedural rationality.

[24] Feng et al. (2020) assessed 150 factors, Harvey et al. (2016) and Neuhierl et al. (2023) investigated over 300 factors, while Harvey and Liu (2019), Hou et al. (2020) and Bartram et al. (2021) explored over 400 factors. Bryzgalova et al. (2023) drew on 51 factors to test for 2.25 quadrillion models based on those. Beyond the factor zoo, an additional problem relates to the choice of the proper proxy for market performance, since this will be needed as a benchmark to calculate excess market and market-adjusted returns in asset pricing models. If dealing with 300-400 factors sounds onerous enough, one should probably brace themselves before the number of possible benchmarks which can be employed in asset pricing: as a 2018 Financial Times article by Authers (2017) showed, there exist over 3 million equity indices. The number becomes even more astounding considering that the total number of publicly listed companies worldwide is less than fifty thousand.

the efficiency hypothesis would render it impossible to assert in which of those sub-hypotheses the root of inefficiency lies.

Another issue surfaced with the Grossman-Stiglitz paradox (Grossman and Stiglitz, 1980); according to this, if the market is efficient and all information (including insider information) is reflected in the price, then no one has an incentive to expend resources to gather information and trade on it. If this holds, the question then arising is how/whether it is possible for all information to be reflected in the price. If, for instance, we assume a trader in possession of costly inside information (costly in terms of both its collection and its legal repercussions–in case he is prosecuted for trading on it), it is hard to fathom that he will incur that information's costs without the possibility of being compensated by profitably trading on it; this is one example, whereby market efficiency (in this case, its strong form) cannot apply. As a result, Grossman and Stiglitz (1980) showcased that informationally efficient markets constitute a practical impossibility.

While the above criticisms were based on analytical-theoretical frameworks, research also saw the emergence of a series of empirical criticisms levelled out against market efficiency. Much of this research focused initially on calendar/seasonal anomalies[25], as well as on the presence of anomalies in stocks of specific features (e.g., size and value effect).[26] Ball and Brown (1968) documented the presence of a post-earnings-announcement drift in stock returns (supportive of underreaction in securities' prices). Shiller (1981) and LeRoy and Porter (1981) showcased that stock market prices are far more volatile than could be justified by a rational model (assuming constant discount rates), thus suggesting that prices entail noisy components, something further elaborated on by Black (1986). Mehra and Prescott (1985) argued that equity returns command a premium over risk-free investments over and above what risk-aversion would warrant, while further evidence denoted that stocks exhibit short-term continuation (momentum; Jegadeesh and Titman, 1993) and long-run reversals (DeBondt and Thaler, 1985).

---

[25] Examples of such anomalies include the January effect, the Monday effect, the weekend effect, the holiday effect and the turn-of-the-month effect, to mention but a few key ones. For more on those, see Lakonishok and Smidt (1988) and Plastun et al. (2019).

[26] Size effect was initially documented by Banz (1981), who reported higher expected returns for small versus large capitalisation stocks; Lakonishok et al. (1994) demonstrated that high (low) book-to-market stocks tend to out(under)perform in future periods.

1.2 Behavioural finance

The systematic unearthing of empirical anomalies/regularities in the 1980s focused researchers' attention to explanations beyond the realm of neoclassical finance, with the focus shifting to evidence from cognitive psychology and decision science from previous decades.[27] This gradually gave birth to a new interdisciplinary research domain, behavioural finance, which primarily challenged neoclassical finance's key assumptions of rationality and arbitrage.

1.2.1 How behavioural finance challenges rationality

1.2.1.1 The 2-System paradigm

As per the debate on rationality, behavioural finance has largely relied on a two-system representation of the human mind (Camerer et al., 2005; Kahneman, 2012); contrary to the neoclassical finance paradigm, where rationality was assumed to be key, the two-system representation assumes that humans can entertain two distinct decision/thinking modes, one that is more "intuitive" (reflexive) and one that is more "rational" (reflective).[28]

The intuitive system (also known as "System 1") is largely uncontrolled (residing outside awareness/consciousness) and involves automatic, reflexive responses, generated with little/no effort.[29] System 1 resorts to automatic processes, which are relevant to solving evolution-related problems (e.g., issues of survival), without necessarily adhering to logical principles (Ardalan, 2018). These processes are rapid, operate in parallel, and, hence allow for multitasking. Relying on patterns retrieved from associative memory, System 1 hinges heavily on habits and impressions to find shortcuts for problems and is prone to emotions. As it relies on heuristics, rather than analytical processing, it aims at passing judgement about people/things/situations, rather than engage into deeper reflection of those (hence being easy to jump to conclusions). Examples of tasks performed by the reflexive mind include driving a car and avoiding a food associated with unpleasant past side-effects to us.

---

[27] For more on how this cross-fertilisation of finance and psychology/decision science research took place initially, see Kahneman (2012).

[28] See Camerer et al. (2005) for a discussion of earlier literature involving alternative versions of similar 2-system models.

[29] Since automatic processes rely on long-established habits/reflexes, we are unable to scrutinise them (they are embedded in our psyche and performed unconsciously) or develop introspective insight into how we decide/judge based on them.

The reflective system (also known as "System 2"), is largely controlled and deductive, processing information analytically/slowly and with effort (following a series of rules), without emotions interfering with this process. Unlike System 1, it treats every thought, concept, person or object with no assumptions, thus maintaining self-control. System 2 uses controlled processes (Camerer et al., 2005; Ardalan, 2018), which are serial (i.e., follow clearly demarcated steps), deliberate (they are used when encountering a novel/special challenge/situation) and are subject to introspection (being aware of controlled processes, we can describe them). Examples of tasks performed by the reflective mind include building a portfolio of stocks and calculating mortgage payments under alternative rates.

Overall, human behaviour in this setting is viewed (Kahneman and Frederick, 2002) as the outcome of an interaction between controlled and automatic processes[30]; whereas controlled processes are the products of more recent biological evolution in humans (they involve computational/analytical skills), automatic processes rely on more primitive brain strata (as they involve elements of affect and intuition).[31] [32] [33] System 1 is the brain's

---

[30] The relatively nascent interdisciplinary domain of neurofinance has proposed an expansion of the 2-system model into a 4-system model; according to the latter, controlled and automatic processes intersect with cognitive and affective ones. For a detailed presentation of this, see Camerer et al. (2005).

[31] This hinges on what is known as the "triune brain"; according to this, the human brain is divided into three regions that correspond to different stages of its evolutionary development, namely the reptilian (focusing on the organism's basic survival functions), the mammalian (focusing on social emotions) and the hominid (focusing on more cognitive/analytical processes) brain. For more on this, see Camerer et al. (2005), Peterson (2014) and Desmoulins-Lebeault et al. (2018).

[32] Controlled (System 2) processes can often transition into System 1; deliberative tasks that are performed repeatedly can prompt our brain to automate their processing. See Ardalan (2018) for more on this.

[33] Systems 1 and 2 need not necessarily be at odds. If both systems generate the same answer to a problem, System 2 will actively endorse System 1's judgement; if, however, System 1 is wrong and System 2 fails to detect it, then System 2 will passively endorse System 1's judgement. In this setting, both types of endorsement (active; passive) imply a connection between error-detection and error-correction. An interesting example of a third perverse interaction between the two systems is presented by Risen (2016). Exploring how humans respond to superstitions, she proposes the acquiescence model. I will present it here in some detail to showcase how the interaction between the two systems is anything but simple. To begin with, superstitious intuitions hail from System 1, as long as System 2 says so; if System 2 is (not) activated, those intuitions can be tackled (prevail). The question therefore is whether System 2 will intervene to correct the false beliefs emanating from superstitions and motivate the individual to reject them. For this correction to take

"default mode", since deliberation can be very taxing for the brain, requiring concentration and, hence, effort. To the extent that it competes for attention and cognitive resources with the rest of the brain's tasks, thinking taxes the mind, more so because it is neurologically "expensive" (about a quarter of our caloric intake is needed to keep the brain running; Forsythe, 2009). As this suggests that thinking is costly, this adds to the costs of decision-making, prompting humans to apply thinking only up to the point where its costs do not exceed its benefits. In turn, this suggests that we do not incorporate all available information into our decisions, which, as a result, are not optimal.[34] This forms a first serious challenge to rationality (and, *in tandem*, market efficiency): if investors do not utilise all signals they can from their informational environment, this denotes that their trades will not reveal all available information. Consequently, market prices will not incorporate all relevant information either, thus compromising a market's efficiency.

System 1 is particularly influential in our understanding of the world, a process mediated by several tools. To begin with, it is important to bear in mind that we live in a signal-rich world, which we cannot cognitively capture/process in its objective entirety;[35] what we do perceive is a truncated, selective version of it, filtered by a series of perceptional factors

---

place, System 2 has to recognise that superstitions are wrong, i.e., detect an error in our thinking mode. If this error is (not) detected, then there exists (no) error-correction. In this case, System 2 can i) correct a false belief (superstition) or ii) endorse it, either because it thought it to be correct, or because it failed to notice that it is wrong. Risen suggests that acquiescence can introduce a third form of "endorsement": System 2 detects the error of System 1's superstition, but does not correct it, thus acquiescing to superstition, even though it knows it to be false. In this case, error-detection and error-correction are decoupled, thus casting doubt over the assumption that detection of an error leads people to correct it; in this specific case, we can maintain superstitious beliefs, even though we realise they are irrational. See Risen (2016) for more on this.

[34] Of course, attaining the optimal outcome need not always be the case in the first place; it may be that optimising is not possible or that the computational costs of optimising are disproportionately high, leading to a negative net cost-benefit outcome. As a result, there exist cognitive limitations, in terms of both knowledge and computational capacity, that introduce boundaries to the rationality of individuals–a concept that came to be known as "bounded rationality" (Simon, 1959). According to this, people prefer "satisficing" over optimising, since what is important is to satisfy the drives of our actions, not to attain an optimal outcome.

[35] Although the human brain can capture around 11 million pieces of data per second, only about 40 of them will be consciously processed (Konnikova, 2013).

(Konnikova, 2013).[36] As a result, much of our attention is motivated, depending largely on which aspects of the world trigger our perception's focus. Even if, however, our attention allowed us improved powers of reception, a second obstacle arising would be one of storage: our memory is subject to flaws that hinder us from proper recollection–or even accurate recollection. Memory fails in two domains, namely content (what recollections I have managed to store) and structure (how I have stored them), and this leads to errors in memory-performance (Konnikova, 2013); it also leads to motivational encoding (the situation whereby we remember things better when we are interested and motivated) and motivation to remember (when we remember what we want/think is important to remember). Taken together, the above suggest that both attention and memory are motivated, thus implying that each of us possesses their own map of reality; as we are not all equally motivated to see the same things in the same way, what we end up observing is not THE reality, but OUR reality. System 1 uses a host of tools that shape our motivated perception of our environment; some of these tools affect the reception of signals from our environment (they are known as "biases") and others affect the processing of these signals (they are known as "heuristics").

1.2.1.2 Biases and heuristics

Biases are psychological forces that distort our perception/reception of signals from our environment. A bias resembles a tinted glass: you know there is something behind it but you cannot see it clearly. This may be either because of limitations in human perception or the way in which a situation is presented. Assume for example a company that has been posting positive earnings for the past eight quarters and that in this quarter posts negative earnings. How would you react to this? There is no singular right (or wrong) answer here. One possibility would be to sell the stock, either for fundamentals-related reasons (if you believe the negative earnings to signify adverse information about the prospects of the company) or behavioural ones (e.g., because you panic). It is, however, equally likely that you will hold onto that stock, since the current quarter of negative earnings will be

[36] These factors include (Konnikova, 2013): coincidence (if a stimulus reminds you of a past experience involving a similar stimulus, hence capturing your attention; you then extrapolate the outcome of the past experience to the present); relevance (a stimulus that is relevant to you for some reason, will capture your attention); subjectivity (a situation can capture your attention, if you believe it to match your beliefs); exclusivity (not paying attention to information because of neglect); and engagement (when "flow" makes you immerse in a task with full attention).

viewed within the frame of the eight previous quarters' positive earnings (the current negative earnings will appear as something close to a blip in an established trend of positive earnings). The latter would be reflective of *conservatism bias* (more on this shortly) and would be a function of how you would be framing your picture of the company's earnings. Let us now add a bit more information into this example, by assuming that earnings in each of the previous eight quarters hovered within the £50,000-£100,000 region and the losses in the current quarter are equal to a negative £1,000,000. Clearly, this magnitude of losses would be salient enough to capture your attention more vehemently, increasing the likelihood of you selling the stock[37]; as a result, how a problem is framed can affect our responses to it, by motivating the surfacing of different biases into the decision-making process.[38]

Heuristics, on the other hand, represent innate processes that affect how we process information. They constitute rules of thumb that have been acquired via (largely reinforcement) learning over the years and form cognitive algorithms operating automatically, without us being aware/conscious of them (Hirshleifer, 2015, 136). Primarily deployed when dealing with obfuscated choice problems, they offer shortcuts towards easy/satisfactory (though not optimal) solutions. Imagine, for example, that you want to build a portfolio of 10 stocks from the S&P500 index-universe; choosing 10 from among 500 stocks is obviously not an easy task and clearly merits some rule that will justify the selection-process. To facilitate this process, the human brain can come up with various shortcuts; in this case, you can: focus on the 10 largest S&P500 index-constituents in terms of capitalisation; pick up the 10 names from the index-list you recognise; pick up the first 10 stocks from that index mentioned in the Wall Street Journal today; pick up yesterday's top 10 performing S&P500 index-constituents; ask your financial advisor; ask your wife/husband etc. Although none of these shortcuts are likely to be ideal in helping you construct the optimal portfolio, they are each capable of simplifying the selection-process, thus denoting that heuristics help provide satisficing, yet not optimal, solutions.

The following example will help demonstrate how biases and heuristics can lead individuals to deviate from rationality. Assume stock ABC and suppose that its price has been rising for a few weeks in a row; you treat this as a trait representative of a good stock and, hence buy it. This is reflective of the *representativeness heuristic* (Kahneman and Tversky, 1972): drawing on a limited sample of observations (a few weeks' prices), you generated

[37] Conversely, if the current quarter's earnings were a meagre negative £10,000, you would be likely to pay far less attention to it.

[38] This, in turn, violates the invariance principle mentioned earlier.

inferences about the population of observations (the stock is good).[39] Let us now assume that the stock's price keeps rising and after some time it experiences a couple of days of negative returns; it is likely that after such a long spree of positive returns, you may view one or two down-days as a blip, downplaying their importance. If so, this is reflective of the *conservatism bias* (Edwards, 1982), which implies slow updating of your beliefs in view of newly incoming information.[40] There is, of course, the possibility that the large (small) number of price rises (falls) prompts you to think that it is more likely that the stock will eventually start falling and, hence decide to sell the stock in advance. This will be motivated by an extrapolative belief in mean-reversion, a belief more formally known as *gambler's fallacy* (Barberis and Thaler, 2003).[41] Of course, before any of the above-mentioned psychological forces kick in, you will first have to identify your window of reference; in other words, which sample of past prices (past one, two, three etc. weeks) do you choose to focus on? This suggests the presence of *anchoring* (Tversky and Kahneman, 1974), which is about extrapolating from some reference point when having to form a judgement. *Availability bias* (Tversky and Kahneman, 1974) can further impact your judgement: if you have been through an event salient enough in your past investment history that looks similar to the stock's recent price movements, this will prompt you to judge stock ABC based on your

[39] As Hirshleifer (2015, 147) argued with respect to representativeness, "People assess the probability of a state of the world on the basis of how typical of that state the evidence seems to be. This is reasonable if typicality is a proxy for the conditional probability of the evidence given the state of the world." In the context of the specific example mentioned here, the stock's surge in price for a few weeks does not have to be a typical proxy for the stock being a good pick. In reality, a good stock does not necessarily have to document such a spree for a few weeks–nor does a stock rising for a few weeks have to qualify as good. An additional issue, of course, here is defining what constitutes a "good stock". As a result, this helps showcase the key implication of the representativeness heuristic, namely that it prompts people to see patterns–and overreact to recent information.

[40] The implication of the conservatism bias is underreaction (in effect, momentum) in the market, since it will take longer for new information to be incorporated in prices. It also distorts Bayesian updating, since, by downplaying information incongruent with the perceived trend, it hampers investors' learning process.

[41] In gambler's fallacy, people view short sequences of events as representative of long ones; as a result, if the stock's price has been rising for a few weeks, you may believe that a reversal is imminent, since in a longer sequence (e.g., a 10-year price-series), rising prices are followed by falling ones.

experience from that prior event.[42] If your past investment experience has been positive, you are likely to ascribe it to your skills (*self-attribution bias*; Barberis and Thaler, 2003); this is expected to breed *overconfidence* (Kahneman, 2012) in the process, rendering it more likely that you will invest in stock ABC without much analysis of its prospects.[43]

Biases and heuristics are important because our everyday life is complex–and they help make it easy by allowing for quick assessment/judgement, which is far easier (and less effortful/time-consuming) than understanding. Being key tools of System 1, they help substitute difficult questions with easy ones (Kahneman, 2012), thus reducing the cost of thinking and rendering decision-making more tractable.[44] Drawing on biases and heuristics, behavioural finance shows that the Economic Man is an abstract concept, with humans in reality being prone to projecting behaviour replete with cognitive errors, not always/necessarily informed by rationality. In other words, rationality is only one possible state/tool of human behaviour that we use–but not all the time. Behavioural finance, therefore, brings finance a step closer to market reality, by showcasing that people: behave the way they behave, not the way we expect/want them to; can be both rational and irrational; can be rational up to a point (they can switch gears); and may be irrational even if they know how to be rational, if it is to their benefit.

---

[42] E.g., you have bought a stock based on its short-term price-rally before and you made/lost a very large amount of money–something not too easy to forget.

[43] Reinforcement learning (Strahilevitz et al., 2011) is also relevant here: a positive experience with an activity is likely to positively reinforce its choice and render it more likely to be repeated. In that spirit, a negative investing experience would be assumed to make you refrain from investing in stock ABC; however, this need not necessarily be the case. If your negative past experience occurred a long time ago, it may be hard to recall (or you may recall it in a biased way that makes it look less negative to you); moreover, even if you do recall it, you may choose not to refrain from investing (thinking that no two investing experiences have to be the same). All of the above cases would be consistent with distortions in learning processes–and, hence, in violation of Bayesian updating.

[44] An example of a difficult question is "How likely am I to lose money by investing in Bitcoin?"; clearly, enumerating the probability of a loss is not easy and would merit consideration of Bitcoin's high volatility, enhanced speculative potential etc. One way to circumvent this problem is to substitute this question with an easier one, like "How many of my friends have lost money investing in Bitcoin?", which reduces the problem to a less cognitively taxing one.

1.2.1.3 Prospect theory

As mentioned earlier, investors in the neoclassical finance paradigm hinge on expected utility theory to compare different alternative choices/gambles; drawing on all possible outcomes of each choice/gamble (and each outcome's probability), the investor calculates its expected utility, before choosing among different alternatives. As a result, expected utility's frame is broad, since it draws on the universe of possible outcomes for each choice-problem. In reality, of course, people are unlikely to be aware of all possible outcomes and/or their corresponding probabilities; being prone to satisficing (than optimising), they are more likely to employ a narrower, less involved, frame to assess their choices. Enter here prospect theory (Kahneman and Tversky, 1979), which proposes that, rather than focus on end-wealth (as expected utility theory would require), individuals assess each choice's outcomes as losses and gains defined relative to a reference point. An interesting depiction of this is presented in Lowenstein et al. (2008, 651):

> "Consider, for example, a gamble that offers a 50% chance of winning £20 and a 50% chance of losing £10. If your current wealth totals £1 million, then [expected utility] assumes that you view the gamble as offering a 50% chance of experiencing the utility of £1,000,020 and a 50% chance of experiencing the utility of £999,990. […] However, as originally noted by Markowitz (1952) and developed more fully by Kahneman & Tversky (1979), people typically make decisions with a more local focus; they "bracket" their decisions more narrowly (Read et al. 1999). Most people would, for example, not view the gamble just discussed in terms of different final levels of wealth, but would instead process it as presented— as a 50% chance of winning £20 and a 50% chance of losing £10."

This narrower frame of assessment is supported by what came to be known as mental accounting (Barberis and Huang, 2001), which refers to the fact that people set up separate mental compartments for different choices/outcomes. Examples of such mental compartments with respect to a person's monetary resources include "kids' college fund", "household management money", "holiday money" etc; key here is the assumption that money cannot be channelled across those mental "budgets" (i.e., it is non-fungible; e.g., money from the "kids' college fund" cannot be used to help finance the family's next holiday). As partitioning their funds into mental "budgets" involves narrow framing, this leads individuals to encode a separate payoff (gain/loss) for each budget; this is clearly at odds with neoclassical finance (which presumes that individuals maintain a comprehensive view of their outcomes), yet does help people tackle potential self-control problems (the case e.g., of individuals dipping into a stock's dividend to finance their needs, without selling the stock to satisfy the latter; see Kahneman, 2012 for more examples on this). In terms of investing, mental accounting would presume that an investor holding a portfolio of stocks views each stock separately (rather than her portfolio as a whole), thus being able to label each stock as a "winner" or a "loser", contingent on its performance (instead of looking at the performance of their portfolio).

Prospect theory posits that, far from maximising end wealth (as expected utility theory would presume), people maximise a weighted[45] sum of utilities determined versus a reference point. The presence of this reference point allows for the encoding of outcomes as gains and losses, and models people's behaviour based on how they value changes in wealth (rather than states of wealth).

More formally, prospect theory's value function assumes the following forms for:

a) Gains: $v(x) = x^\alpha$ for $x \geq 0$, $0<\alpha<1$

b) Losses: $v(x) = -\lambda(-x)^\beta$ for $x<0$, $\lambda>1$, $0<\beta<1$

Here, x is the amount of change in wealth (positive or negative, reflective of gains or losses, respectively) and v(x) denotes the value that the investor places on it. Its graphical representation is depicted in Figure 1-1 and highlights how changes in wealth are treated asymmetrically, depending on their sign. As the graph suggests, the function is concave (convex) in the domain of gains (losses), bearing a kink at the origin. That kink is the result of the value of λ; since $\lambda > 1$ indicates loss-aversion, the values that λ assumes (2.25-2.5) in prospect theory (e.g., Tversky and Kahneman, 1992) denote that a £1,000 loss is equal to, in absolute terms, a £2,250-2,500 gain (or, equivalently, that the loss of x is around twice more painful than a gain of x is pleasurable). This denotes the presence of loss-aversion, namely a greater sensitivity to losses than to gains. The fact that the value function is steeper for the area of losses than that of gains further indicates that gains prompt people to sell more quickly (to pocket their profits, since waiting might lead those gains to evaporate)[46], while losses

[45] The weights used ("decision weights") are not true probabilities, but rather subjective representations of probabilities, resulting from a satisficing process. According to this process, extremely unlikely (likely) events are treated as impossible (certain), while small/large (moderate) probabilities are overweighted (underweighted). See Sapra and Zak (2008) for more on this.

[46] Gambler's fallacy can motivate such expectations, as it implies that gains will eventually have to revert; also, if a winning stock starts losing, people can experience regret (for investments made out of choice) or disappointment (for investments made

prompt them to hold onto their positions for longer (in anticipation of a reversal).[47] More formally known as the reflection effect (Kahneman and Tversky, 1979), this denotes that gains (losses) motivate risk-averse (risk-seeking) behaviour.

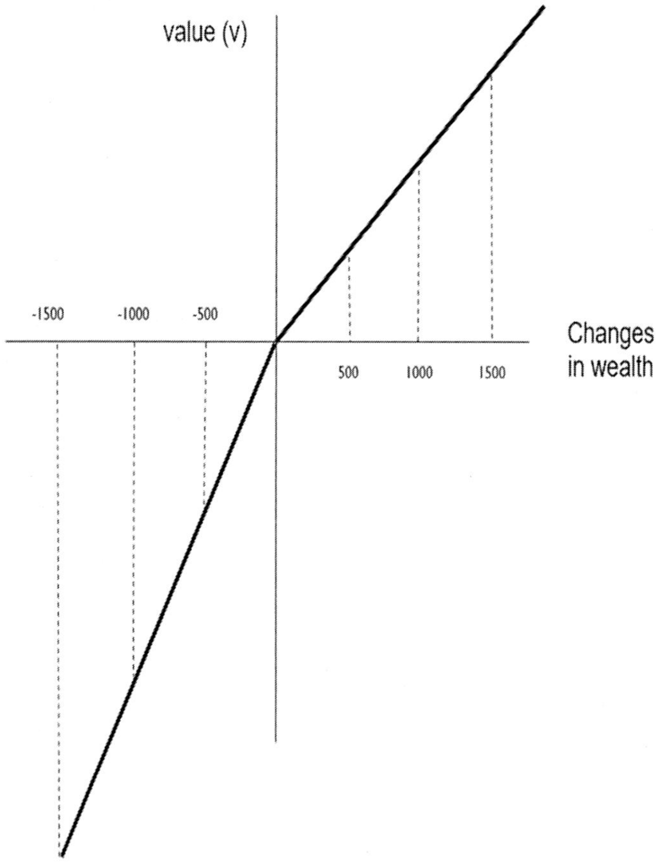

Figure 1-1: Prospect theory value function.

---

not out of choice) for not selling it earlier. Barberis and Xiong (2012) explain this via realisation utility: investors derive positive utility from selling a winning stock, preferring realised (over paper) gains, because they help enhance their self-esteem.

[47] Again here, gambler's fallacy would suggest that losing stocks will eventually rebound (thus justifying holding onto them); also realising losses would derive negative utility to the investor (Barberis and Xiong, 2012), who would experience a loss in self-esteem by realising them.

Prospect theory has been found to be much more representative (compared to expected utility theory) of the way people reach decisions in real life.[48] It also shows how the axiom of continuity is violated in actual decisions: the fact that we are risk-averse (risk-seeking) in the domain of gains (losses) suggests that the same problem can generate diverse choices depending on how it is presented (thus confirming the role of framing in choices). The introduction of prospect theory helps demonstrate how deviations from rationality can, beyond the reception and processing of information, also affect the way people formulate their decisions. Our discussion has so far showcased how behavioural finance challenges rationality, one of the key pillars of neoclassical finance. In the next subsection, we will show how it challenges another one of those pillars–arbitrage.

1.2.2 Limits to arbitrage

Neoclassical finance presumes that the realisation of any mispricing in the market will be tackled by rational investors via arbitrage. If, for example, an asset is overpriced (underpriced), an arbitrageur would go short (long) on it, while at the same time go long (short) on a similar asset underpriced (overpriced) in the same/a different market.[49] Though intuitively plausible in principle, reality might challenge its feasibility. To appreciate why this may be the case, we need to explore some real-life conditions introducing costs/risks to arbitrage.

To begin with, when arbitraging a stock's mispricing, it is important to be able to hedge your bets, in case the mispricing assumes proportions rendering arbitrage unprofitable. If, for example, you believe a stock to be overpriced, it would make sense to go short on it in anticipation of its reversal; if, however, its price-rally continues (e.g., because good news keeps arriving about the stock), shorting the stock would lead you to realise losses. To mitigate this, you could go long on a similar stock that is underpriced, since you would expect its price to rise in the future. For this to happen, two things (at least) should hold: first, the similar stock must be a "close substitute" (i.e., entail similar cash flows/fundamentals, and belong to the same sector as the stock you are trying to arbitrage); and second, it

[48] The case e.g., of situations whereby people exhibit path-dependence, reference-dependence, frame-dependence, ambiguity-dependence and emotion-dependence in their preferences. See Baltussen (2009).

[49] Or the same asset traded in a different market (e.g., a dual-listed stock).

must not be mispriced itself.[50] Since neither is guaranteed in capital markets (close substitutes need not exist for every stock, nor are they immune to mispricing), this will give rise to *fundamental risk* and reduce the feasibility of arbitrage (Shleifer and Vishny, 1997).

Second, to be able to tackle mispricing, one has to be able to practice arbitrage without frictions; examples of those frictions include transaction costs (e.g., brokerage commissions), short-selling costs, taxes (e.g., capital gains' or transaction ones), liquidity risk (the case e.g., of thin trading delaying order-execution), legal/regulatory provisions (e.g., restrictions in short-selling and margin trading for foreign investors in some markets), and collateral/funding constraints.[51] Amid such *implementation costs*, arbitrage grows more costly–and hence, less potent in tackling mispricing.

Implementation costs can be further detrimental to arbitrage when combined with prolonging of the mispricing–more formally known as *horizon risk* (Barberis and Thaler, 2003). To the extent that arbitrage is not costless, trying to eliminate a mispricing that persists for a very long period of time will likely lead arbitrageurs to see their profits eroded by the costs associated with the implementation of arbitrage.

Since arbitrage is costly/risky, an arbitrageur may consider practicing it, if she sees enough of her peers doing so too. If a sufficiently large number of investors engage in arbitrage, this will lead to a quicker dampening of a mispricing, thus encouraging more arbitrageurs to join them. If, on the other hand, an arbitrageur sees limited arbitrage activity in the market (or is uncertain as per how many others investors are willing to arbitrage), she may decide it is preferable to pursue other trading strategies, instead of arbitraging.[52]

A key factor rendering arbitrage riskier is *noise trader risk* (De Long et al., 1990b). Initially coined by Black (1986), the concept of noise traders constitutes one of the building blocks of behavioural finance and refers to investors who trade for reasons other than information. Assumed to be of low sophistication (and, hence, primarily identified with retail investors;

---

[50] If the close substitute stock's underpricing persists (instead of reverting), then buying it would lead you to realise losses.

[51] See the discussion in Shleifer and Vishny (1997), Barberis and Thaler (2003) and Dávila et al. (2022).

[52] This has been dubbed (Barberis and Thaler, 2003) "*synchronisation risk*" (since it involves uncertainty as per how/whether arbitrageurs will be able to synchronise their trades to tackle mispricing). If this risk is high, (some) arbitrageurs may deem it preferable to ride on the mispricing (e.g., some of them may trend-chase). For more on this, see Abreu and Brunnermeier (2002; 2003) and Brunnermeier and Morgan (2010).

Barber et al., 2009), noise traders are unlikely to rely on fundamentals (and equally less likely to process them rationally, even if they had access to them), preferring to trade on noise (i.e., non-information) instead. Although noise traders contribute to market liquidity[53] (thus rendering it more feasible–and, potentially, profitable–for informed investors to trade on their information), their presence can also impound noise into prices. Therefore, the higher the presence of noise traders and the more correlated their deviations from rationality[54], the more likely it is that mispricing will occur and be of greater magnitude. This is bound to be an issue for arbitrageurs, since they normally hail from the delegated money management industry and any prolonged mispricing is likely to hurt their funds' performance. If a fund manager trying to arbitrage amid elevated noise trader risk underperforms, his investors may feel ambivalent about his skills and qualities, potentially considering selling their shares in his fund. To ensure his clients remain invested with his fund (and thus safeguard his career prospects), the fund manager may end up moderating/suspending his arbitrage activities.[55] The regulatory framework of the fund management industry adds a further dimension to the above: fund managers are subject to periodic (quarterly to semi-annual) performance evaluation versus their

[53] In view of the established (Karpoff, 1987; Gallant et al., 1992; Jones et al., 1994) positive correlation between volume and volatility, the higher volume motivated by noise trading also helps exacerbate volatility–thus leading prices to depart from their fundamental valuations. This suggests noise as an explanation for the excess volatility findings of Shiller (1981) and LeRoy and Porter (1981) mentioned earlier; it also denotes that volatility need not only be due to prices responding to information (e.g., Ross, 1989), but can also be the result of noise in the market.

[54] Aside from retail investors' susceptibility to behavioural biases (Barber and Odean, 2013), the latter can also motivate correlation in their trades; see e.g., Dorn et al. (2008), Barber et al. (2009), Sicherman et al. (2015), and Arnold et al. (2022).

[55] Fund managers have been found to be very sensitive to their clients' risk-appetite, in order to ensure they retain them as clients (Chelley-Steeley et al., 2019). If arbitrage leads a fund manager to underperform, his clients are unlikely to support the risks accruing with arbitrage to the fund and may well respond by moving their money to other funds. This is entirely rational and follows from the agency relationship between fund-investors ("principals") and fund managers ("agents"), since the fiduciary responsibility of the latter towards their clients is to ensure the best possible management of their clients' wealth, not ensuring prices are efficient in the market. Rationally choosing his career security over bringing prices closer to fundamentals, the manager will then moderate/suspend his arbitraging activities. Of course, managers can also choose to implement strategies riskier than they otherwise would, if the prevailing sentiment in the market raises investors' risk-appetite (Frazzini and Lamont, 2008); this is the case e.g., with funds increasing their exposure to stocks with lottery features (Agarwal et al., 2022).

peers, hence any evidence of underperformance can place their career prospects in jeopardy. What is more, to the extent that fund managers' performance is often benchmarked against a given index, this suggests that what is important to them is to track/beat the index, not arbitrage away any of its deviations from fundamentals (Baker et al., 2011).

An additional factor rendering arbitrage risky is *model-risk*. If an arbitrageur relies on an asset pricing model, which he believes to be misspecified, he will treat its arbitrage signals with scepticism, potentially being less eager to arbitrage based on those signals. It is also likely that he will only choose to arbitrage, if the expected returns from his arbitrage trades are above a certain threshold (i.e., sufficiently high enough to compensate for his model's uncertainty). This would be very similar to the findings of Maenhout (2004), who showed that model-misspecification can prompt investors to demand higher premia from equities.

The above suggest that arbitrage is likely to face obstacles and frictions in capital markets that can dampen its impact and practice–and lead mispricing to survive. Although part of this mispricing is due to noise investors (see e.g., Brogaard et al., 2022), part of it is also the result of sophisticated traders not harnessing arbitrage's full potential (due to its costs/risks). Much empirical evidence[56] is broadly supportive of this, thus denoting that arbitrage should not be viewed as a given in capital markets. In addition, concerns have been raised[57] over the role of arbitrage in promoting inefficient pricing, thus indicating that its contribution to market efficiency is not as guaranteed as envisaged by neoclassical finance.

---

[56] Textbook cases of limits to arbitrage include the evidence presented by Froot and Dabora (1999) and De Jong et al. (2009) on dual-listed companies. For a broader discussion on arbitrage, see Dávila et al. (2022). See also Stambaugh et al. (2015) for a discussion and evidence on arbitrage asymmetry, i.e., the fact that it is easier to go long on an underpriced than short on an overpriced stock.

[57] Hirshleifer (2015) argues that, arbitrage can dampen mispricing, as long as it is practiced by investors who are both rational and do not cater to noise traders' sentiment. The latter is important, given how rational speculators can either exploit (De Long et al., 1990a) or succumb to (De Long et al., 1990b) sentiment, allowing prices to temporarily depart from fundamentals. Another issue with arbitrage is its potential to give rise to overcrowding (Ülkü and Onischchenko, 2023); defined as excess trend-chasing following information releases, overcrowding can lead prices to overreact, reaching levels over and above those implied by information. As a result, this culminates eventually in price-reversals and an increased probability of crashes. The authors attribute overcrowding to excessive arbitrage activity (which is more than that actually needed for prices to converge to fundamentals) and ascribe this to fund managers tracking their peers' trades in order to avoid underperforming their peers (or their industry's benchmark).

1.3 Concluding remarks

This chapter has presented the key pillars of the neoclassical finance paradigm (Economic Man; market efficiency) and their underlying features and assumptions, before outlining the objections of behavioural finance to those. Behavioural finance proposes a paradigm of investors' behaviour informed via cognitive psychology, demonstrating that humans bear limitations, in view of the presence of psychological factors introducing distortions in the reception (biases) and processing (heuristics) of information. These limitations challenge the notions of the Economic Man and market efficiency, leading to a calibration of investors' behaviour more closely aligned with reality. These limitations also suggest that the formation of prices need not strictly follow fundamentals–nor that any deviation of prices from fundamentals can always be arbitraged away.

The debate from the behavioural finance side has been ongoing at least since the 1980s, largely based on foundations borrowed from research conducted in psychology and decision science since earlier decades. How does *Confusion of Confusions* fit into this context and how does it qualify as history's first known primer on behavioural finance? Before addressing these questions, I will first present the background to Joseph de la Vega, his community and the stock exchange setting which motivated the write-up of his book.

CHAPTER 2

CONFUSION OF CONFUSIONS: BACKGROUND

Confusion of Confusions is set in a context involving the Amsterdam Stock Exchange, following its launch via the initial public offering of the Dutch East India Company in 1602. Its author is also positioned within that context (being an active trader in that stock market, as well as a merchant), with the community to which he belonged (Sephardi Jews) playing an active role in Dutch international trade–and trading in the stock exchange itself. This chapter provides a detailed presentation of the above. Section 2.1 focuses on the evolution of Sephardi migration across Europe in response to changes in international trade following their expulsion from Spain in 1492 and how they traced their steps to Amsterdam. Section 2.2 discusses aspects of their community's organisation in the Dutch capital. Section 2.3 introduces the Dutch East India Company (world's first publicly traded joint stock company); its establishment marked the birth of the Amsterdam Stock Exchange (world's first organised stock exchange), which is presented in section 2.4, with several details as per aspects of its trading dynamics. Section 2.5 presents a short biography of Joseph de la Vega, while section 2.6 provides a brief introduction to (and overview of) *Confusion of Confusions*.

2.1 The Sephardi

2.1.1 Origins

The term "Sephardi"[58] refers to those Jews hailing from the Iberian Peninsula, with historical sources tracing their presence in the region as far

---

[58] The term stems from the Hebrew "səpharad" (Hebrew: סְפָרַד), which was used to allude to the region of modern-day Spain. As mentioned in Obadiah in the Bible: "And the captivity of this host of the children of Israel shall possess that of the Canaanites, even unto Zarephath; and the captivity of Jerusalem, which is in Sepharad, shall possess the cities of the south." (Obadiah 1:20)

back as the 1st century AD, with their influx growing following the destruction of Jerusalem by the Roman Emperor Titus in 70 AD.[59] Overall, their community's fortunes on the peninsula exhibited ebbs and flows, largely determined by shifts in the peninsula's dominant religion. Flourishing during the break-down of the Western Roman State, their community endured its first persecutions following the adoption of the Christian faith by the Visigothic royal family in the late 6th century–persecutions which continued well into the start of the 8th century, until the onset of the Moorish invasion of Spain and the establishment of the Al Andalus kingdom (Assis, 1988). The latter witnessed an improved position for Sephardi Jews (several of whom were assigned key posts in the kingdom's administration), a fact which continued for the next three centuries (Roth, 1994). The breakup of the kingdom in smaller provinces and the gradual switch of power to less tolerant forces (Almoravids; Almohads) shifted the tide for Sephardi populations, who began being viewed with increased hostility (Stillman, 1979; Gampel, 1992). As the *Reconquista* (the reconquest of the Iberian Peninsula by Christian forces) picked up in pace since the 11th century, the Sephardi began to offer their administrative services to the incoming Christian forces; however, as the reconquest progressed, they were often subject to mixed treatment (often viewed as accomplices of the Moors' conquest), depending on the prevailing ruler of each province (Biale, 2012).

A pivotal moment in Sephardi history corresponds to the concurrent pogroms against Jews in several Spanish cities during the 1390s, which culminated in a surge of forced conversions of Jews (Michael, 2006). The number of converts (*"conversos"*) probably amounted to more than half of the size of the Sephardi community, giving rise to a new social segment, the so-called "New Christians" ("*nuevo cristianos*").[60] Their convert-status was hereditary, with a christened child of a convert retaining the convert's status for life (Held, 2006). Their ranks swelled over the 15th century, with many of them secretly practicing their ancestral faith (Kaplan, 1981).

The apogee of those persecutions is identified with the Alhambra decree; issued on March 31st, 1492, it called for the expulsion of unconverted Jews (and Moors) from Spain within three months (i.e., by July 31st, 1492), leading a large number of unconverted Jews to seek passage to safe lands

---

[59] Also known as the "Destruction of the Second Temple" (the First Temple having been destroyed when the Babylonian king Nebuchadnezzar II conquered the city of Jerusalem after a prolonged siege in 587 BC). For more on this and some evidence on the ancient Jewish presence in Spain, see Flavius Josephus (1981; 2023).

[60] Also known as "*marranos*" *and* "*anussim*" ("the forced ones"). For more on them, see Pérez (2007).

(Kaplan, 1981). Initially, many chose to flee to neighbouring Portugal (hence, they began to be known as "Portuguese Jews"); the introduction, however, of conversion decrees during 1496-7 and the Inquisition in 1536 in Portugal[61] prompted many of its *conversos* and unconverted Jews to migrate (De la Vega, 1957). Of those, many headed for religiously more tolerant destinations in Europe (e.g., Amsterdam, Hamburg, Bayonne, Livorno), a large fraction chose to migrate to the Ottoman Empire, while some ventured towards non-European destinations (e.g., in the newly discovered lands in the Americas).[62]

2.1.2 Sephardi migration to Amsterdam

The 16th century witnessed a surge in international trade, as a result of the Discoveries already underway since the 15th century. This led to the evolution of transatlantic trade between the countries involved in the Discoveries and their newly founded colonies. For the most part, this included routes toward South and East Asia, as well as toward the Americas. Of particular interest to this book is the North-South corridor of traffic, which entailed trading routes connecting North-Western European ports with the evolving colonies of the Spanish and Portuguese Empires in Central and South America. The corridor's southward route focused on the export of products (primarily from England, Flanders, France and the Netherlands), including fish, spices, cloth, timber, Baltic grain, linen, wheat, rye, flax, iron, copper, tar, lead, and hemp. The corridor's northward route, on the other hand, aimed at importing products from Spain, Portugal and their evolving colonies into Northern Europe; said products included raisins, bullion, cochineal, indigo, tobaccos, wools, olive oil, sherry wine, fruits, salt, colonial dyestuffs, sugar, sumac, and figs.[63] Much of this trade passed through Spanish ports in the Canary Islands, Southern (Cadiz; San Lúcar de Barremeda) and Northern (Cantabrian coast) Spain, with Seville functioning as a hub for the insurance/financing of this trade.

How do Sephardi Jews fit into this North-South traffic? In simple terms, their migration-directions following their expulsion from the Iberian Peninsula were largely determined by changes in the importance of various import/export points in that traffic. In general, when Sephardi

---

[61] The Inquisition had been launched since 1479 in Spain with the purpose of ensuring the eradication of non-Christian faiths from the country (Trivellato, 2017).
[62] See the discussion in Davidi (2019a).
[63] The above list of products of both routes draws largely on Swetschinsky (1981, 61). For more on the North-South traffic, see Israel (1978; 1980).

Jews picked up migration-destinations, they based their choice primarily on two factors: first, whether these destinations were religiously tolerant (Klooster, 2001); and second, whether they harboured good commercial prospects. To the extent that they were dispersed in different locations across the then known world, they formed a set of trading networks, which their host countries strived to exploit, given the growth in international trade at the time.

A key first application of their networks in trade took place after the large migration of many Sephardi Jews to the lands of the Ottoman Empire after 1492. Through their brethren in Venice, they managed the import-export trade in spices between Venice and the Ottoman Empire (Klooster, 2001). A second window of opportunity presented itself with the 16th century discovery of maritime routes to India by the Portuguese, a discovery that essentially put Portugal as a key player on the global map of the spice-trade. The connections maintained by the Sephardi Jewry with the Portuguese Crown allowed them to capture the trade of spices as well as other products brought from the Portuguese colonies, particularly Angola, Brazil and Goa, while also entering Spanish trade with the Americas (Klooster, 2001).[64]

The networks they nurtured, therefore, allowed the Sephardi Jews to develop a commercial model that contributed to the integration of distant markets across several continents. Much of the success of their networks has been attributed (Sutcliffe, 2007) to the enhanced trust such networks

[64] This was primarily accomplished via *conversos* from Portugal and was particularly evident during the period when Spain and Portugal were under a single Crown (1580-1640), when many Portuguese *conversos* relocated to Madrid and Seville to partake in Spanish colonial trade by setting up commercial and banking houses; see the discussion in Klooster (2001) and Trivellato (2017). One should also note here that, besides goods, Sephardi merchants were also involved in the trafficking of slaves from Spanish/Portuguese colonies in Africa to Spanish colonies in the Americas via exclusive contracts (*asientos*) with Spain since as early as 1595. For more on this, see Klooster (2001) and Schorsch (2005); see also the references on this issue in Israel (1978) and Swetschinski (1981).

fostered, as well as Sephardi Jews' flexible political loyalties.[65,66] As a result, far from being centrally coordinated, Sephardi business activities were built around commercial kin-based business networks. Kinship was quintessential in ensuring trust in a very uncertain cross-border business environment and involved forging business associations with relatives and close friends, who would act as business partners, factors, brokers, or agents in trading posts across the world that served specific trade routes (Swetschinsky, 1981).

A major immigration destination–in view of the Netherlands' evolving importance in international trade–for the Sephardi was Amsterdam, with their migration pattern to the city proceeding in fits and starts from the mid-1590s until the 1670s. To offer some background on the political-economic conditions of the time, we need to note here that the entry of Amsterdam as a key player in the global commercial stage did not commence before the 17th century. In the 16th century (1500-1585) it was Antwerp that constituted a major entrepot for international trade, as it was the key European distribution centre for merchandise and precious metals from European colonies. As Israel (1989) mentions:

> "…the handling and distribution of Portuguese and Spanish colonial products was heavily concentrated there. In Antwerp were the factors who corresponded with Lisbon, Oporto, and Seville, the warehouses where high-value colonial merchandise was stock-piled, and the sugar-refineries, diamond cutters, and other specialists in the processing of colonial wares" (Israel, 1989, 46)

---

[65] Such flexibility was necessary amid the uncertainties permeating domestic (in terms of their host country) and international political and economic conditions, since variations in those uncertainties affected the trade routes available. Flexibility was further warranted in terms of traded products, since long distance commerce involved "routes" more than "products" (implying that one traded the products available on the route, not the products of one's choice; Swetschinsky, 1981). On the issue of their political flexibility, see also the following from Sutcliffe (2007, 435): "Indeed, it was in large measure the mobile allegiances and malleable cultural identities adopted by crypto-Jews and New Christians living under Catholic rule that enabled the Sephardim to sustain trade across the most entrenched barriers of religious and imperial rivalry."– see also Trivellato (2017, 157-158).

[66] Such network structures would be expected to also have resulted in lower transaction and information costs; with respect to the latter, this was further rendered possible by the fact that toll farming in Spain and Portugal was largely in the hands of *conversos* (who could thus easily share privileged information on the flow of trade with their brethren through their network). See the discussion in Klooster (2001, 128) and Cardoso (2002, 111).

Antwerp initially flourished as a result of the concentration of major banking houses of the time (primarily German, but also Italian ones–who had migrated from nearby Bruges) there, motivated by the Portuguese spice trade, which was channelled through the city (in exchange for copper and silver) since the early 1500s. This rendered Antwerp a major depot for several other colonial wares (spices, precious metals, and sugar, among others), whose distribution and processing involved the heavy participation of its Sephardi community. The city's prosperity continued unabated throughout the first half of the 16th century. By the middle of that century, the Portuguese trade with the city began to scale back (mainly due to the discoveries of large gold mines in Peru–which, thus rendered trading in gold easier via nearby Spain), yet an enhanced trade with Spain began. This was driven by the Spanish expansion in the Americas, which necessitated the import of products from Northern Europe into Spain and its colonies. The year 1557 witnessed a recession kicking in (largely the result of many of the city's bank-defaults), with a partial revival in the mid-1560s (motivated largely by the textile industry). A key issue that led to the downfall of Antwerp was the fact that it was located in the so-called "Spanish Netherlands"[67], a region which was in a state of conflict with the Dutch state. The Spanish recapture of Antwerp from the Netherlands in 1585 sealed the city's decline; as the river Scheldt, the city's sole sea access, was blocked (its estuary was Dutch-controlled), the city could not fulfil its prior commercial functions (Israel, 1978; 1989).[68]

The aftermath of the Dutch-Spanish conflict of the time saw the imposition of a Spanish embargo to Dutch trading with Spain, Portugal and their colonies (1585-1590); the embargo plunged the Netherlands into a recession, leading to the emigration of many of its merchants–and the shifting of much of its trading activity to north-western German cities (Cologne; Hamburg), Bordeaux, Rouen and London (all of which were within close geographical proximity to Antwerp and maintained direct trade links with Portugal and its colonies). Of all those destinations, Hamburg benefited the most, becoming (during the 1585-1595 period) the centre of the sugar, spice and other colonial commodities' distribution in northern Europe, leading to a boost in the city's sugar-refining and attracting substantial Sephardi immigration (Israel, 1989).

The 1590s proved more auspicious for the Dutch state; as the Spanish embargo was lifted in 1590, Dutch trading activity began to pick up. Much

---

[67] Corresponding largely to the bulk of modern-day Belgium and Luxembourg, alongside parts of modern-day France, Germany and the Netherlands.

[68] For a more detailed discussion of Antwerp's economic history in the 16th century, see Mosselaar (2018).

of this was due to the Portuguese trade, with Portugal seeking to import cereals (as it got hit by bad grain harvests) and export its colonial products. Given Antwerp's port blockade since 1585, this trade was gradually (after 1590) diverted to Amsterdam, which–equally gradually–began overtaking Hamburg as the main European port in colonial goods' distribution (Swetschinski, 1981). This development prompted an initial influx of Sephardi Jews into Amsterdam during the 1590s, marking their first migration wave to the Dutch capital.[69]

The 17th century entered on a negative note for the Dutch state, as a ten-year embargo was imposed against it in 1598. The embargo included trade with Spain, Portugal, and Spanish territories in Europe (including the Spanish Netherlands and Spanish Italy); to mitigate the embargo's adverse effects on Dutch overseas trading, the Dutch responded by organising their own long-distance trading missions since 1598 to Asia, Africa and the Caribbean, while also establishing some sugar plantations in Northern Brazil (Israel, 1989). Though beneficial, these failed to gain the Dutch a firm foothold in the sugar-trade, which, post-1598, was channelled through Europe via Portugal, and then directly to Hamburg–which thus regained its primacy in sugar distribution in Europe. On top of that, the Anglo-Spanish peace treaty of 1604 further opened up Portuguese trade to England, thus adding to the competition for the Dutch in this trade (Israel, 1989). As a result, this motivated migration on behalf of Sephardi merchants outside the Dutch Republic and toward locations (e.g., London, Rouen, and Emden) which could offer their commercial operations easier access to trade with Portugal under the new circumstances (Israel, 1989; Klooster, 2001).

This second embargo came to an end in 1609, when the 12-year Truce was signed between the Spanish and the Dutch. As expected, this development positively impacted the Dutch economy, as the Dutch began to dominate the broader North-South corridor. As Dutch spices (among other goods from the colonies) began to be freely traded in the Iberian Peninsula and Spanish dominions (including the Spanish Netherlands and Spanish Italy; Gelderblom et al., 2013), this led to enhanced Dutch-Spanish trade, with Dutch exports being paid with Spanish bullion; the latter, in turn, was used to finance the build-up of the Dutch army and navy (Israel, 1978). The economic boom that ensued, prompted a second influx of Sephardi merchants into Amsterdam, leading Sephardi communities in Northern Europe to gradually fade away (Koen, 1970). However, this trend reversed when the 12-year Truce expired in 1621 and the embargo was reinstated

[69] Beyond Portugal, many Sephardi came from Venice, Antwerp, Germany, France and Brazil (Israel, 1989).

(largely due to Spanish dissatisfaction with the strengthening of the Dutch Republic at Spain's expense, as they saw it).[70] The embargo adversely affected the Dutch economy and had a strongly negative impact over the commercial operations of Sephardi merchants; the latter began departing from Amsterdam and settling down at other trading ports in Europe (mostly, yet not exclusively, in Germany) to bypass the embargo (Israel, 1989).[71]

A key milestone in the Dutch effort to secure part of the sugar-trade was the occupation of North Eastern Brazil by the Dutch West Indies Company in 1630 (Israel, 1978); the first settlements in that region were established in 1634 and lasted until 1654 (when Dutch Brazil effectively collapsed; Klooster, 2001). The establishment of Dutch Brazil fomented–for the first time-direct trade between the Netherlands and Brazil, a trade which was largely handled by Dutch Brazil's Sephardi community (Trivellato, 2017); the latter experienced significant prosperity during the 1630s and 1640s, thus prompting the migration of Dutch-resident Sephardi to Dutch Brazil (Swetschinsky, 1981).

The Portuguese war of independence in 1640 brought forth further disruption (as well as opportunities) for Sephardi merchants. On the one hand, it adversely affected Sephardi operations in the Spanish colonies. Part of the problem was that many *conversos* handling the Spanish trade with the Americas were from Portugal (from where they had returned to Spain since the 1580s); as a result, Portuguese independence focused political and economic suspicion on them (as potential collaborators of the Portuguese) and motivated Inquisition activity.[72] On the other hand, however, the

---

[70] As Israel (1978) mentions: "It was this rapid accumulation of Spanish bullion in the republic which Spanish ministers saw as the fundamental cause of the massive enlargement of the Dutch land and naval forces during the truce, the alarming spread of Dutch influence and subsidies in Germany and Italy, and the intolerable impetus of Dutch colonial investment and enterprise. Moreover, the [Council of the State] was convinced that the trade balance was being made still more unequal by means of various illegal methods such as abuse of grain-importing licenses, evasion of customs duties, and the smuggling into Spain, in return for silver, of counterfeit Spanish copper coinage forged in Holland." (Israel, 1978, 3)

[71] For more on how this embargo was not particularly strictly enforced (and how the Dutch tried to bypass it), see the discussion in Israel (1978).

[72] As Swetschinsky (1981) notes, those suspicions were anchored on multiple angles: first, on the joint business ventures of Portuguese *conversos* with Amsterdam Sephardi; second, on the connections of Spanish-resident Portuguese *conversos* with those residing in Portugal; and third, on the possibility of those relations motivating contraband (e.g., Dutch importation of goods from Portugal and its colonies, disguised as Dutch merchandise into Spain). The latter suspicion was very real, in view of evidence of Dutch Jews acting as intermediaries in the silver trade between

breakaway of Portugal from Spain in 1641 boosted Dutch commerce with Portugal, with the latter needing Dutch support (in weapons' supplies) in its independence-struggle. As a result, the trade relationship between Amsterdam and Portugal shifted now in favour of Amsterdam; to the extent that the Dutch could now exploit Brazil both directly as well as through their trade with Portugal, this exploitation could best take place from Amsterdam, thus resulting in another influx of Sephardi merchants there, mostly from Hamburg and Antwerp (Swetschinsky, 1981).

The 1648 Dutch-Spanish peace treaty of Münster saw the lifting of the Spanish embargo, resulting (once again) in the dominance of Spanish trade by Sephardi Jews.[73] This was largely supported by the strong presence of *converso* (and associated *non-converso*) merchants in Spanish ports.[74] The 1650s, however, witnessed a fundamental change in the trade of Sephardi Jews with Brazil; the siege of Dutch Brazil by the Portuguese (1645-1654) and the concomitant collapse of Dutch Brazil in 1654 signified the decline of trade between Holland and Portugal (with the role of the English growing more important in the Portuguese trade; Israel, 1978). Seeking safe passage, many members of the Dutch Brazil Sephardi community migrated to Dutch trade stations in and around the Caribbean (Curaçao; Barbados; Jamaica; Surinam/Dutch Guyana), with many also fleeing to the Netherlands (Swetschinsky, 1981; Israel, 1989; Klooster, 2001).

However, it was events in Spain that further helped accelerate Sephardi/*converso* migration to the Dutch Republic. In 1647, Spain declared bankruptcy (Israel, 1989), amid a period entailing multiple wars (that had strained government finances), trade depression (following the dampening of transatlantic commerce), bad harvests, famine and plague (Israel, 1978; 1989). As the above conditions rendered raising taxes hard, the Spanish Crown (with the help of the Inquisition) scapegoated tax farmers

---

Spain and Portugal during the 1640-1665 Spanish-Portuguese war, as well as engaging into arms smuggling (Israel, 1980). To mitigate suspicions against them, Amsterdam Sephardi merchants used non-Sephardi brokers (primarily British and Dutch) when trading in Spanish colonies and resorted to using Dutch aliases during the 1650s to deflect attention away from their "Portuguese" origins.

[73] This involved a series of restrictions; for example, Dutch Jews could enter Spanish trade not directly (but only through non-Jewish factors) and were prohibited from physically entering Spain (Israel, 1980).

[74] The Sephardi presence in Northern Spanish (Basque; Cantabrian) ports has been justified through those ports' proximity to Madrid, where a large number of wealthy *converso* merchants/financiers were located–and for business with which, *non-converso* associates were used by Dutch Jews as intermediaries (Israel, 1980).

(who implemented state taxation–and most of whom were *conversos*).[75] This led many *conversos* from Portugal who had migrated to Spain after 1580 to leave the country; many of them settled in Amsterdam and helped shift new capital to the Netherlands (considering that many were financiers and tax-farmers). The Venetian-Turkish war (1645-69) further destabilised Sephardi Venetian trade, with many Venetian Sephardi choosing to migrate mainly to Livorno and Amsterdam (Israel, 1989). Overall, successive Sephardi migration waves culminated in growing Sephardi numbers in Amsterdam and other Dutch cities that peaked by 1672 (Israel, 1989).

2.2 The Amsterdam Sephardi community

The first Jewish migrants to the Netherlands were Sephardi, primarily from the Iberian Peninsula[76], who spoke Portuguese and who, as a result, came to be known by the Dutch as "Portuguese" or "Portuguese Jews" (Sutcliffe, 2007). Kaplan (1981) mentions that the bulk of their community comprised of *conversos* (or *conversos'* descendants) who returned to the faith of their ancestors. The Sephardi settled primarily in main Dutch urban centres, including Amsterdam, Rotterdam, and Middelburg and were welcomed by the Dutch, as they were viewed

> "[…] as economically useful, as bringing expertise and connections in spheres of commerce which were not yet established in the Dutch entrepôt but which were seen as important for its further expansion" (Israel, 1989, 45)

A key reason for choosing the Netherlands as their destination was that the country offered an environment that was more liberal and with fewer restrictions, compared to other countries at the time. Unlike in other European countries, Jews encountered comparatively fewer restrictions in terms of settlement and movement; they experienced no ghetto conditions, while any restrictions toward their migration were city-specific (Amsterdam

[75] This included the Spanish Crown reneging on its agreements with *converso* financiers and expropriating their assets. To the extent that the business of many of them was linked with Antwerp, the fortunes of the latter also declined then. For a detailed presentation of the above, see the discussion in Israel (1978, 47-56).

[76] As mentioned in the previous sub-section, many of them also hailed from non-Iberian lands, including, Belgium, France, Germany and even the Americas (with most of them, in effect, shifting locations contingent on the changing circumstances of international politics and trade).

placed no such).[77] They also experienced religious freedom (Schöffer, 1981); the first Jewish cemetery was established in Ouderkerk/Groet in 1614[78], while a large synagogue (known as the "Portuguese Synagogue") was consecrated in 1675 in Amsterdam.[79]

In terms of organisation, the Sephardi community in Amsterdam[80] followed a community-governance model similar to that of their brethren in Venice's Ponentine[81] community (Israel, 1989). Their community was headed by a council (*"Ma'amad"* or "*mahamad"*)[82] of seven elders (*"parnassim"*)[83], who were entitled to choose their successors; they hailed from families of considerable wealth and were entrusted with the community's governance and the payment of the bulk of its taxes (Held, 2006). The Amsterdam Sephardi community evolved out of three distinct congregations (Kaplan, 1989): *Beth Jacob* (established sometime between 1597-1602); *Neveh Shalom* (established sometime between 1608-1612); *Beth Israel* (est.

---

[77] For more on this issue, see Israel (1978) and Schöffer (1981). Restrictive settlement laws did apply for Jews in the Netherlands (abolished in 1795 with the Emancipation; Schöffer, 1981).

[78] The cemetery was originally bought by the Venetian Sephardi nobleman Isaac Abeniacar (Portuguese alias: Don Manuel Pimentel), who was also the first person to have been buried there in 1615; he was the brother of Mordechay Abeniacar (Portuguese alias: Garcia Pimentel), one of the very first Sephardi to settle in Amsterdam in the mid-1590s from Venice. The cemetery's registry *Livro de Bet Haim* (*"Book of the House of Life"*) is a vital source of information for the community's past. For more on the above, see Koen (1970) and Israel (1989).

[79] Evidence of the first religious gatherings of Jews in the Netherlands dates back to 1602-1603, with rabbi Uri-ha-Levi performing the first services (Koen, 1970); an initial application for building a synagogue to Haarlem City council was filed by Jews of Venetian roots in 1604 (Israel, 1989). The Amsterdam synagogue ("*esnoga*") was constructed during the 1671-1675 period.

[80] The focus here is on the Amsterdam Sephardi, given that they constituted at least half of all Sephardi residing in the Netherlands (see Nusteling, 2002). The English-language literature reveals comparatively less evidence as concerns Sephardi communities outside Amsterdam.

[81] The term "Ponentine" was used in official documents of Italian cities welcoming Sephardi as a term referring to *conversos* from Iberian lands (as opposed to "Levantine", which was used to refer to Sephardi of proper Jewish faith from the Ottoman Empire). See Trivellato (2017, 139).

[82] The term was originally used in the ancient times to denote those men appointed to observe standing (from the Hebrew verb עמד, *amad*, meaning "to stand") the communal offerings in the Temple Courtyard in Jerusalem. These men would therefore "stand over" the sacrifice to pray, while the latter was offered. See ben Maimon's Klei Hamikdash, Chapter 6:1.

[83] "Shepherds", "stewards".

1618)[84]. These congregations formed an umbrella organisation (*Impost Board*; 1622-1639), with the purpose of collecting the "*imposta*" (import/export tax) and providing for the needs of the community (particularly those of its poorer members, who needed to travel abroad; Koen, 1970); by 1639 the three congregations had merged into a single congregation (*Talmud Torah*).

The community catered to several aspects of its members' welfare. As early as 1616, the Beth Jacob community set up the *Talmud Torah* school to offer *conversos* instruction in matters of their ancestral faith. The school maintained its own library (*Ets Haim*), with both the library and the school later coming to be known as *Ets Haim* (*Tree of Life*).[85] In addition, the community's authorities exhibited keen interest in advancing adult education, particularly in religious doctrinal matters via oral and written means.[86] In 1615, the community set up the "*Santa Companhia de Dotar Orfas e Doncelas Pobres*"[87], which aimed at the financial support for marital purposes (i.e., dowry) of poor orphans and maidens. The society attracted several wealthy members of the Amsterdam Sephardi society (as well as Sephardi merchants from overseas); preference was given to girls of Iberian roots with no financial means.[88] Further funds designated to aid underprivileged members of the Sephardi community included the *Sedaca* for the poor and *Abi Yetomin* for orphans (Heertje, 2015). One thing the community became staunch about (since 1644) was to forbid its members to travel to countries where the practice of Judaism was proscribed (such as e.g., Spain), possibly to prevent them from being tempted in terms of their

---

[84] A spin-out of Beth Jacob; see Koen (1970, 38).

[85] *Ets Haim* was a religious school (*yeshiva*), whose curriculum focused on the study of Hebrew, the Torah, and the Talmud (Davidi, 2019b). As Goldish (2001, 12) mentions, the school's system was based on the principles of Comenius and other educational reformers of the time. A key contribution of the school to Jewish culture at the time is that it supplied rabbis (from among its best pupils) for various Sephardi communities internationally; its reputation rested largely on its competitive admissions policy and rigorous instruction, rendering it an elite educational establishment for several centuries (Dweck, 2019).

[86] The outreach towards adult members of the community involved a mix of compilations/translations of religious works in Spanish and Portuguese, coupled with sermons during synagogue masses, where moral issues were expounded in a clear/succinct fashion, in order to facilitate their absorption by those in attendance (Goldish, 2001, 14).

[87] "*The Sacred Company to Provide Dowries to Orphans and Poor Maidens*".

[88] For more details of the selection process of dowry-eligible orphans/maidens, see Swetschinsky (1981) and Roitman (2005).

religious convictions (as they would be expected to pretend to be *conversos* in such countries). As Kaplan (1981) mentions:

> "[...] the leaders of the Portuguese community [...] in 1644 enacted a regulation that obliged all members of the community who, after returning to the "lands of idolatry", came back to Amsterdam, to be called up to the Ark in the synagogue and ask publicly for forgiveness; the regulation also forbade them to fulfil any public function in the community during the first four years following their return" (Kaplan, 1981, 43)[89]

Although the Sephardi faced far fewer restrictions in the Netherlands (compared to other countries), this by no means implies that restrictions were absent at all. A host of decrees stipulated discriminatory treatment for Amsterdam Jews, who, for example, could not take up occupations practiced by members of the city's guilds, join a guild, or set up a retail shop. They could, however, practice non-guild related occupations; among the latter, one could identify occupations directly or indirectly related with the colonial trade (e.g., diamond-cutting; wholesale trading; shipping; brokering; money market), so one might argue that this worked both to their advantage (due to their expertise in those professions) as well as the advantage of the Dutch authorities (who thus exploited their expertise). Sephardi Jews could not hold public office, while attainment of citizenship (*"burghership"*) neither allowed them to practice guild-related occupations, nor was it hereditary.[90]

---

[89] Although this last example suggests the presence of rigidity among the religious leaders of the Sephardi community, such rigidity exhibited flexibility in its expression, for various reasons. To begin with, the community comprised largely of ex-*conversos*, many of whom possessed a certain intellectual caliber, which often prompted them to challenge religious authorities/traditions. In addition, Amsterdam's Portuguese Jews viewed their affiliation to the "Portuguese Nation" (as they called their community) in terms that were more ethnic than religious (thus implying that they treated *conversos* who did not revert to Judaism as kin). As a result, the community entertained a dichotomy of sorts: while it viewed the synagogue as "sacred", it interpreted Jewish law with greater laxity when coming to matters of everyday life; in turn, this motivated conflict with rabbinic authorities, particularly rabbis of non-*converso* background (who would experience a lesser connection with the background of their synagogue's members). For more on this, see Goldish (2001).

[90] In retrospect, this was similar in nature to the acquisition of the Christian identity by *conversos* in Spain-which could not be passed further down the family line by parents who had been christened; New Christian parents' christened children were treated as New Christians, not proper members of the Christian faith (see section

In view of those restrictions, the Sephardi focused their activities in areas primarily related to merchandise trading[91], brokering, as well as diamonds, among others.[92] In addition, the Sephardi community set up a number of Jewish publishing houses (Berger, 2001) and produced some emblematic scholarly figures in philosophy (Baruch Spinoza) and economic theory (Isaac de Pinto). All in all, the Amsterdam Sephardi constituted a small, yet vibrant, community, which never exceeded a few thousand members; though estimates vary, they hover between 3,000 and 7,000 for the end of the 17th century (see e.g., Nusteling, 2002, Sutcliffe, 2007, and Nogueira, 2017).[93]

2.2.1). For a detailed discussion of the restrictions the Sephardi faced in Amsterdam, see Koen (1970).

[91] In line with what we mentioned in the previous sub-section, much of the Sephardi's' merchandise trading was based on kinship-networks, often involving Amsterdam merchants and corresponding merchants in Spanish and Portuguese ports. As Swetschinsky (1981) discusses, these cross-border trade partnerships tended to be run from Portugal, not Amsterdam, with Amsterdam Sephardi Jews primarily focusing on contracting maritime insurance for transatlantic voyages.

[92] Nogueira (2017)'s statistics, for example, reveal that among the Amsterdam Sephardi in the year 1743, there were over 200 merchants, over 120 brokers and about 30 specialists in jewellery/diamonds.

[93] Apart from the Sephardi community, Amsterdam also gradually began to acquire an Ashkenazi Jewish population from Central-Eastern Europe. Initially, they were known as "German-Jews" (having migrated during/following the Thirty Years' War of 1618-1648); the first cohort among them were German/Bohemian Jews, who migrated to Amsterdam in the 1630s. Amsterdam's Askhenazi community was first established in 1635 and became an independent juridical entity in 1639. A further influx of Lithuanian/Polish Ashkenazi in the Dutch capital ensued following the 1648/9 pogroms in the Baltics/Poland and the 1654 war between Russian/Sweden and Poland. The Lithuanian/Polish Ashkenazi (some of whom were converts) established their own community in 1660, before merging into the earlier Ashkenazi community of Amsterdam in 1673. After 1670, the Ashkenazi community ceased being under *mahamad's* control. Sephardi Jews viewed their Ashkenazi brethren with some ambivalence. On the one hand they helped them financially, via the *Avodat Hesed* (*Merciful Works*) *Society* established in 1642. On the other hand, however, they hastened to finance their departure to overseas destinations, largely due to Ashkenazi's widespread poverty rendering settling down at Amsterdam (with its high cost of living) prohibitive. To that end, the *Impost Board* financed their transportation to various destinations (including Baltic ports, the Ottoman Empire, as well as Dutch colonies). For a detailed discussion of Ashkenazi migration to Amsterdam and Sephardi attitudes towards it, see Kaplan (1989).

2.3 The Dutch East India Company

The growing expansion of the Dutch Republic's international trade during the 17th century rendered the country Europe's leading economy (Gelderblom and Jonker, 2004).[94] The naval ventures of Dutch merchants, while previously confined to continental European ports[95], started to gradually expand to transatlantic destinations. As Dutch merchants began focusing on larger-scale (and -distance) journeys, the need for cooperation among them (in the form of company partnerships) became more pressing. Larger trading expeditions needed more financing, entailed higher risks (e.g., in terms of delays or lost ships) and merited longer-term capital commitment (any profits to investors could only be distributed upon the safe return of a ship).[96] On top of that, deposits or bonds (in the form of IOUs or bills obligatory) were insufficient to cover the costs (Gelderblom and Jonker, 2004).

An initial attempt at tackling this issue surfaced in the late 16th century in the form of early trading companies (*Voorcompagnieen*). The latter comprised special-purpose (i.e., formed to commission a single voyage) partnerships, whereby the directors undertook all necessary voyage-preparations (crew, provisions etc.) largely based on financing obtained from investors who paid cash up front (Gelderblom et al. 2013).[97] Upon the ship's safe return, the directors sold the cargo and liquidated the company's assets, in order to cover up any remaining costs, set aside a fraction of the proceeds for their fees, and distributed any residual amount left to investors. The above arrangement presented, however, an issue: since investors' claims were only tied to a singular ship/voyage, there was really no guarantee that they would be willing to participate in future operations (more so given the financial underperformance of the initial voyages).[98] The experience of the *Voorcompagnieen* clearly indicated to the Dutch that

---

[94] For more on the drivers of the Dutch economic boom in the 17th century, see Cardoso (2002, 110).

[95] For example, Kaplan (1989) mentions that around 2,400 Dutch ships were engaged in trade with the Baltics in the first half of the 17th century.

[96] For more on this, see Jonker and Sluyterman (2000).

[97] Investors in *Voorcompagnieen* were liable only to the extent of their share-participation in the specific voyage; although this limited liability extended to directors for their equity participation as well (Gelderblom and Jonker, 2004), they did bear unlimited liability for any debt contracted by them to finance the company (*ergo*, debt was personal, not the company's; Gelderblom et al., 2013).

[98] *Voorcompagnieen* tended to run on negative flows prior to 1602 (see Gelderblom and Jonker, 2004).

securing ongoing financing was a necessary precondition for the continuation of transatlantic voyages.

To resolve this issue (and boost Dutch presence in transatlantic trade), the States General of the Dutch Republic[99] tried to get all companies involved in such voyages to cooperate, instead of compete with one another. To that end, the Dutch East India Company[100] (*Vereenigde Oostindische Compagnie*, or VOC for short) was founded in 1602 through the participation of the various trading companies of the Netherlands' six chambers (*kamers*)[101] of East Indian trade (Amsterdam, Delft, Enkhuizen, Hoorn, Middelburg[102], and Rotterdam), each of which retained a fixed share in the company's operations. The company's charter (signed by the States General) was drafted on March 20th, 1602 and provided for a company, whose life would last for 21 years, during which it would enjoy a monopoly in the country's Asian trade (Mosselaar, 2018). It also provided for the liquidation of the company within ten years (by 1612)[103], at which time its shareholders could then re-invest their money in the successor company, which would exploit the rest ten of the monopoly's years.

As the company was under the oversight of the States General (Gelderblom et al. 2013), the latter strived to utilise it to further Dutch military-commercial interests overseas; to that end, the Dutch government contributed to the equipment of company-ships with guns and artillery, with the company paying for naval defensive convoys and mercenaries out of its profits. Throughout its lifespan, the Dutch East India Company established forts, factories and local governments in Asia[104] and Africa and had a broad

---

[99] The States General formed the supreme authority in the Netherlands since the late 16th century, following the rebellion of the northern Netherlands against the Spanish Crown in 1581, that kickstarted a long conflict between the Spanish and the Dutch (Eighty Years' War; 1566-1648). It comprised of representatives of the provincial assemblies ("states") of the Netherlands that had seceded from Spanish rule. See van der Lem (2019) for more on this.

[100] Also occasionally quoted as "Dutch East *Indies* Company" (e.g., Dumez, 2015).

[101] Each chamber represented the merchant stock-owners of the Dutch East India Company of each community; each chamber, therefore, participated in the governance of the company (more on this shortly), with Amsterdam's chamber being the largest.

[102] Also known as the Zeeland chamber (see e.g., Gelderblom et al., 2013); Middelburg was (and still is) the capital of the province of Zeeland.

[103] As per the charter, the company would publish its performance-accounts from its first decade of operations in 1612 and shareholders would then be entitled to a refund of their investment, if they so wished.

[104] In 1619, it captured Fort Jacatra on the island of Java and established its headquarters there, renaming the location into Batavia (Gelderblom et al., 2013).

spectrum of jurisdiction within its remit, as it could: negotiate and sign treaties with foreign sovereigns; appoint governors of territories and cities; coin its own money; set up trading posts (that doubled as local administrative centres; Kroon, 2015), build forts, enlist soldiers and carry out military campaigns. In view of its formidable scale of operations and geographical reach, it ended up being the largest single employer in the Netherlands.[105]

The corporate governance of the Dutch East India Company was based on a board of directors called "*Heren Zeventien*" ("the gentleman seventeen"); members of the *Heren Zeventien* were selected on a rotating basis from among the company's directors (*bewindhebbers*). The latter acted as underwriters for new shares (Gelderblom and Jonker, 2004), were entitled to one percent of every shipment brought to shore by each ship belonging to their chamber (Held, 2006), and were in charge of voyage-preparations for their respective chamber's ships (Gelderbloom et al., 2013). As per the *Heren Zeventien*, they were responsible *inter alia* for policy, price-setting, cross-chamber loans and dividend policy (Gelderblom et al., 2013). The board's composition reflected chamber-representation, with non-Amsterdam chambers retaining a majority of one on the board to deter its dominance by the Amsterdam-chamber (Mosselaar, 2018). In terms of corporate disclosure, it appears to have been rather opaque; to *bewindhebbers*, company financial information was proprietary and thus rarely publicly disclosed, resulting in lack of transparency about the company's finances (Petram, 2014). In addition, there was also the *Haagse Besogne* based in the Hague, which acted as an advisory board to the Dutch East India Company; its composition reflected chamber-representation and its duties involved dealing with the correspondence from overseas outposts[106], and preparing an annual report (*Haags Verbaal*) to the *Heren Zeventien* (Kroon, 2015).

The initial public offering of the company–the first IPO in history–took place during August 1602 (with the subscription-register kept open until the month's end) and proved rather successful. In modern-day terms, the offer price was set at 3,000 guilders and the subscription involved just over 2,100 shares. Investors could subscribe to a whole share or a fraction of it, with no prescribed maximum/minimum amount of investment set (Stringham, 2003). The IPO's proceeds amounted to 6,440,200 guilders, with the Amsterdam-chamber clearly dominating the subscription with around 55-

---

[105] For more on the collaboration of the Dutch East India Company with the Dutch State, see Gelderblom et al. (2013) and Mosselaar (2018).

[106] Specifically, from the authorities of the main Dutch outpost of Batavia.

56% participation in the total capital raised.[107] Subscribers did not have to pay the full price of their shares upfront, but could spread it over four instalments of 25% (due on 1603), 33.3% (due on 1604), 33.3% (due on 1605), and 8.3% (due on 1607). Each of those instalments corresponded to a trading voyage of company ships; although the fourth instalment appears residual, the expectation apparently was that the ships from the first three voyages would return by 1607 and their revenues would be high enough to finance the fourth voyage (Gelderbloom et al., 2013).[108] This suggests that whether a voyage would materialise largely depended on how successful the immediately previous one/s had been; rather than this denoting the presence of a fixed financial base, it indicates a revolving fund replenished conditional on future voyages' revenues (Gelderblom et al., 2013).

The Dutch East India Company's IPO gave birth to the Amsterdam Stock Exchange, where shares of the company could now be traded among investors. Its IPO boosted speculative trading, with its share's price rising by about 15% within the first few days post-IPO (Gelderblom and Jonker, 2004).[109] Suffice to say that by 1607, the price had doubled, while by 1688 (when Vega wrote *Confusion of Confusions*), it had inflated by around 580% (De la Vega, 1957, xv). The company's share-price witnessed several bubbles and crashes throughout its history, attesting to its very high (and speculation-motivated) volatility levels; landmark events in the company's

---

[107] As per Stringham (2003), Amsterdam's chamber contributed with around 3,592,000 guilders to the IPO. The corresponding percentages for the rest five chambers to the IPO's capital were as follows: Middelburg (20%), Enkhuizen (8%), Hoorn (7%), Delft (4%), and Rotterdam (3%). In total, 1,130 investors participated from Amsterdam alone, an impressive number, considering the adult population of the city was estimated at about 50-60,000 at the time (Israel, 1995; Gelderblom et al., 2013).

[108] To encourage early payments to ensure prompt coverage of each voyage's costs, the company offered 8% interest until each voyage's sail to shareholders paying up early; however, this provision seems to have proved unable to cover the funding gap, thus resorting to directors borrowing on the Amsterdam money market (Gelderblom and Jonker, 2004). Gelderblom et al. (2013) offer a different view, arguing that directors preferred borrowing over offering the 8% interest, since they could borrow for less than 8% on the Amsterdam money market. Vega himself alludes to the low borrowing rates of his time, mentioning that secured (unsecured) loans carried a rate of 2.5% (3%) per annum (De la Vega, 13, para 92).

[109] This forms, in essence, the first example of IPO-underpricing in financial history. IPO-underpricing represents the fact that companies offer their shares to the public when listing on an exchange for a discounted price, resulting in the returns of the initial day/s of the IPO being positive, on average. For more on this, see the discussion and references in Duong et al. (2022).

price-history include the tulip mania boom/bust (late 1630s; company ships were also transporting tulip bulbs), the 1672 crash (during the English, French and German attacks on the Netherlands; Mosselaar, 2018) and 1688's Glorious Revolution (see sub-section 2.6).

Although the Dutch East India Company was, indeed, the first publicly traded joint-stock company, it did not operate as a single company from the start. Rather than a proper merger of the six chambers, its initial form was one of a cooperative of independent chambers, something further illustrated by the fact that shares were nontransferable among chambers (e.g., shares traded in Amsterdam were for the Amsterdam chamber only) and priced differently across chambers. As a result, each chamber "kept their capital, and commercial operations separate from each other, while observing general guidelines, and policies, set by the federal board of directors" (Israel, 1995, 321). Consequently, the Dutch East India Company's initial expeditions were chamber-specific, with the prospects of each chamber's future expeditions depending on the success of previous ones.[110] This led to a reduced volume of spices being carried back to the Netherlands (and, concomitantly, low sales-revenues that prevented many expeditions from breaking even)[111], thus not fostering the continuity of Dutch trade in Asia. This was further compounded by the company's dual (commercial; military) duties in the Asian seas; as per States General's instructions, company-ships were often ordered to remain in Asia for tours of duty of several years, in order to engage against Spanish forces there (thus adding to the company's huge operational costs).[112]

The conversion of the Dutch East India Company into a joint-stock company in the modern sense of the term underwent a process of almost two decades. The first step in that direction involved the accounting harmonisation across chambers (1606-1608), following the increase in

[110] Evidence from early voyages was far from encouraging. The Amsterdam-chamber dominated the first expeditions (December 1603-April 1606), supplying around two-thirds of the 32 ships involved. The picture for non-Amsterdam chambers was less positive, since they did not participate in all expeditions. See Gelderblom et al. (2013) for more on this.

[111] With spice-cargoes being still low in the early years of the company, the company had to draw on stockpiled spices from its constituent trading companies to sustain the country in the spice-trade. See Gelderblom et al. (2013).

[112] Long tours of duty produced delays in the return of ships, thus enhancing uncertainty as per the profitability of each expedition; they also increased costs during (e.g., salaries of crews) and after the tour (e.g., cost of repairs/replacement of ships). See the discussion in Gelderblom et al. (2013). The *Heren Zeventien* were not always seconding such decisions (directors' resignations were reported in 1603 and 1605; Gelderblom et al., 2011).

cross-subsidisation of chambers (the direction of which ran mainly from Amsterdam to the rest five chambers), in order to ensure confidence among the chambers in their finances (which, in the process, centralised corporate finance decision-making in the hands of the board).[113] The second step took place in July 1612, when the States General allowed for the company's statutory liquidation to be ignored.[114] The third step was undertaken in the autumn of 1617, when the board declared that it assumed exclusive responsibility for borrowing decisions for the company, thus further centralising corporate finance decision making in the company (chambers now needed permission prior to raising debt). The outcome of this declaration was that chambers' debt was transformed from a personal liability (of each chamber's *bewindhebbers*) into a joint liability of all directors (in effect, directors mutually guaranteed each other's debts). To add credence to this, all directors (and their successors) signed a contract guaranteeing that their chamber's share in the company's future debt would be tied to their chamber's share in the company's capital. The fourth, and final, step can be traced in the renewed charter of the Dutch East India Company in 1622 (which was the year just before its statutory termination). Despite enhanced demands on behalf of shareholders for company accounts to be made public (amid a rise in the company's debt, which suggested high default risk) that year, no such disclosure took place, with the charter

[113] According to this harmonisation, chambers would regularly inspect each other's accounts; also, chambers had to send each other monthly reports and submit statements to each board meeting. See Gelderblom et al. (2013).

[114] The history behind this can be summarised as follows: the revolving fund system coupled with the military duties of the Dutch East India Company could not sustain Dutch presence in Asia, be it commercial or military. Part of the issue may be traced in the fact that the Dutch colonial expansion was more motivated by business opportunity than empire-building (Kroon, 2015, 182). To that end, Navy Commander Cornelis Matelieff de Jonge recommended to the States General in 1609 the establishment of a permanent hub in Asia to help further the company's military and commercial aims. The key obstacle to that was that the company's statutory liquidation was nearing (it was scheduled for 1612); with Asian voyages proving far from profitable, Matelieff was worried that this would deter future investors from financially supporting the Dutch East India Company's successor post-1612 (more so, since the company had also failed to pay any dividends up to that point). To that end, Matelieff recommended to the States General that the statutory liquidation be ignored and the company be turned into a permanent concern. The States General acted on this recommendation 3 years later. The establishment of the permanent hub Matelieff proposed took place much later, with the capture of Fort Jacatra by the Dutch in 1619, following lobbying by J.P. Coen, senior executive of the Company, to the States General. See Gelderblom et al. (2013) for a detailed discussion of this.

renewed on December 31st, 1622. The difference was that now bonds issued by chambers were not personally guaranteed by the directors, but instead were signed off by the company's bookkeepers; this, in effect, terminated the personal liability of directors for the company's debt, rendering the company itself liable for its debt, thus treating it as an independent legal entity.[115]

An issue that proved thoroughly vexing (for the company and its shareholders) over time was the company's dividend policy. With its revolving fund policy of its initial form being unable to cover the expeditions' costs, the company pursued a zero-dividend policy for the first ten years of its life. The first dividends were paid between 1610 and 1612, as a result of Isaac Lemaire's response to Matelieff's recommendation (see footnote 114) on ignoring the company's statutory liquidation in 1612–a response which culminated in Lemaire's bear raid on Dutch East India Company shares[116] and prompted the company's directors to approve a massive dividend during 1610-1612. Despite the size of the dividend (which "represented full reimbursement plus ten times the going interest rate of 6.25 percent for each year their capital had been tied up in the company."–Gelderbloom et al., 2013, 1061), shareholders were far from content with it[117], the reason being that, due to cash shortages, a substantial part of it was to be paid in kind (spices).[118] To allay shareholders' concerns, the board agreed to pay part of the in-spice dividend in cash; as a result, by 1613 the company paid off 3,000 guilders per share in cash, namely the share's offer price of 1602 in full.[119] Over the years, as the company gained in strength,

[115] This was first trialled with bonds from the Middelburg chamber issued in Amsterdam–see the discussion in Gelderblom et al. (2013, 1071).
[116] In effect, the first documented evidence of shareholder activism in equity markets. More than that, Lemaire also approached the French king to ask him to launch a competitor company to the Dutch East India one. See the discussion in Gelderblom et al. (2013, 1061). For more on Lemaire, see the next sub-section.
[117] Gelderblom et al. (2013) produce data suggesting that most investors refused to accept a dividend in spices.
[118] Although the company offered the dividend in spice-form using its own official prices to convert it into cash-terms (Gelderbloom et al., 2013), the excess supply of spices in the Dutch market meant lower prices for them (and hence a lower dividend, in real cash terms; Mosselaar, 2018).
[119] This payment was stretched out over the years; 57.5% of that was paid in 1612 and the rest 42.5% was paid in 1613 (Stringham, 2003). Although shareholders may have been temporarily calmed, there remained a large part of in-spice dividend with an option of being paid in cash by 1616; due to its large amount, it was later converted into interest-bearing loans (Gelderblom et al., 2013).

it managed to pay off a higher dividend (about 22.5% on the original capital per annum, on average; Stringham, 2003).[120]

A relatively under-researched aspect of the Dutch East India Company is its relationship to Dutch social networks. The first type of network involved family-networks; specific families provided the company with employees for several generations. These employees often ended up occupying significant positions within the company in its overseas posts, where they formed their own kinship networks (Kroon, 2015). The second type of networks were the masonic ones; their expansion internationally during the 18th century accompanied Dutch colonial expeditions[121], with the masonic identity of a substantial fraction of VOC-directors/employees having been recently confirmed (Kroon, 2015). The presence of Dutch masonic lodges in Dutch colonial stations/outposts helped form a complex network[122] supporting both state and business purposes, given the importance the Dutch state attached to the Dutch East India Company's presence in Asia.[123]

---

[120] As Vega states in paragraph 18 of *Confusion of Confusions*: "From the founding of the Company to the date of this conversation, the dividends have amounted to 1,482.5 per cent, while the value of the capital has increased more than five-fold." (De la Vega, 1957, 4, para 18).

[121] The Dutch Grand Lodge (the supreme masonic authority of the country) encouraged the establishment of masonic lodges in Dutch colonial territories for influence- (to expand its jurisdiction) and finance-related (to broaden its income base from membership-fees) reasons (Kroon, 2015). Considering that the Grand Lodge was established in the Netherlands in 1735, it did not take long for the first colonial lodges to be founded (1754 in the West Indies; 1759 in the East Indies).

[122] An innovation of the time that helped bolster the dynamics of masonic networks was the issuance of membership-certificates, which confirmed an individual's masonic identity. These helped function as "masonic passports" for individuals travelling internationally, by facilitating mutual aid among freemasons in overseas territories with existing masonic lodges. For more on how masonic passports worked, see Burt (2003), Jansen (2015), and Kroon (2015).

[123] The presence of masonic activity in European colonial empires can first be traced within the British and the French colonial empires. To the extent that lodge-members hailed from a cross-section of social segments heavily involved in colonial projects (aristocrats; military; merchants; mariners), masonic lodges facilitated the bonding (bridging) of people from the same (different) circles, offering a model of sociability in a familiar (since lodges were frequented by their fellow countrymen) environment away from their home countries. Such an environment fostered networking and the exchange of information, both very important to business conduct across colonial empires of the time. For more on this, see Burt (2003), Jansen (2015), and Deschamps (2017a; b).

2.4 The Amsterdam Stock Exchange

The Amsterdam Stock Exchange evolved out of the Amsterdam Bourse, which was initially set up as a commodity exchange in 1530. Physically located in a building modelled after the Antwerp Bourse's building (inaugurated in 1531; see Torisson, 2019) with a capacity of 500, and built during 1608-1611 over the Rokin canal, it grew over the years to become a major market in commodities' futures, offering futures contracts for over 300 commodities (Stringham, 2003).

The Amsterdam Stock Exchange was formally launched in 1602, following the initial public offering of the Dutch East India Company and was the first organised exchange in financial history to offer a secondary market for equity shares of publicly listed companies (for more on the technical evolution of this, see Gelderblom and Jonker, 2004).[124] The reception of this secondary market for equities was rather positive, with speculation on shares documented even before the actual receipt of stocks by their buyers.[125] Indeed, trades on Dutch East India Company shares were registered immediately after its initial public offering, before even the deadline for the first instalment for its shares (1603). As there were no actual shares in circulation pre-1603, but only paper promises, one might surmise that such trades must have involved some futures contracts (Gelderblom and Jonker, 2004).[126]

[124] Although it was the very first organised stock exchange offering a secondary market for joint stock company shares, it was not the first exchange venue for securities, in general, in financial history. Markets for government bonds, bills of exchange and forward contracts existed since the 14th century in various Italian cities; in the 15th century, Bruges offered an *ad hoc* space for merchants from Italian and Hansard cities in its central square near the Van Der Beurse inn (from where the term "bourse", as we know it, was later coined). Antwerp gathered momentum afterward, becoming the world's first international money market on government loans and establishing the world's first organised commodities exchange (1485). The latter pioneered the trade of bills of exchange on underlying commodities (in effect, giving birth to derivatives' trading, with forward contracts on various commodities and precious metals being traded based on those bills). See Stringham (2003) and Mosselaar (2018) for more on the above.

[125] This speculation on stocks has also been ascribed to the Dutch population's familiarity with paper-claims (see Gelderblom and Jonker, 2004, 666).

[126] The success of the secondary equity market, impacted the bond market as well, as Dutch East India Company shares were used as collateral for debt, as early as 1602. This helped keep interest rates low and lowered information and enforcement costs in creditor assessment (Gelderblom and Jonker, 2004). This practice, known

The stock exchange brought together a rather heterogeneous mix of participants. Among the investors existed wealthy capitalists (interested in dividend income), merchants (seeking to hedge their operations) and speculators (interested in profiting from price-differentials)–see De la Vega (1957, 5, para 22). Brokers also existed in this process (be they "official", or "free")[127], as well as "rescounters" (who offered settlement-services for transactions; De la Vega, 1957, 23-24, para 226); key also was the presence of the Bank of Amsterdam (established in 1609), which functioned as the central bank of the Dutch Republic at the time (De la Vega, 1957, xviii).

A peculiar feature of the Amsterdam Stock Exchange's "ecosystem" was the presence of two "syndicates", the "Bulls" and the "Bears", as Vega defines them. The Bears' syndicate was headed by Isaac Lemaire, one of the largest (98,000 guilders) subscribers in the 1602-IPO of the Dutch East India Company; he was also a former director of the company, a post he relinquished in February 1605, following fraud-accusations. All in all, the syndicate of the Bears comprised of a few (8-10) merchants and received support by company insiders; a key example of the latter involves the case of company accountant Barent Lampe who made false entries in the company's share-register (see Mosselaar, 2018). The Bears' syndicate gained in prominence since 1609, when Lemaire protested Matelieff's recommendation to the States General about ignoring the company's statutory liquidation of 1612; Lemaire's response (see previous section) culminated in the first bear raid on the company's shares.[128] The Bulls, on the other hand, comprised of those traders eager to provide support to the company's share-price; although less is known about them, it is perhaps fair to assume that they were affiliated with the company's directors, who strived to keep the Dutch East India Company afloat amid the challenges encountered during the first couple of decades of its life.

Trading hours were not entirely clearly defined. Vega mentions that they involved a morning session (taking place between 10am and 12pm at the

---

as "hypothecation", involved the borrower obtaining a loan whose value could not exceed 80% of the value of the shares pledged as collateral (Stringham, 2003, 332).

[127] Official brokers were members of the brokers' guild and were sworn in by municipal authorities; they could not engage in proprietary trading and were subject to *numerus clausus* (Dumez, 2015). Free brokers (*beunhaas*) carried no license and were allowed to engage in proprietary trading. Their numbers far exceeded those of official ones; for Sephardi brokers alone, Nogueira (2002) shows that free brokers were five times more than official ones (100 versus 20).

[128] Gelderblom and Jonker (2004) estimate the Bears-syndicate's participation in the company's share-volume to hover between 10-20%; though relatively small, it was sufficient to exert price-pressure over the company's shares.

Dam, a square opposite the Amsterdam city hall) and an afternoon session (taking place between 12pm and 2pm at the Exchange building).[129] According to the details offered by Mosselaar (2018), the morning session must have corresponded to the hours during which trades took place among Jewish speculators in their district–followed by the afternoon session at the Exchange. However, there was also some sort of after-hours trading, which took place in investment clubs[130] during evening hours (as well as the Dam Square).

Trading on the Amsterdam Stock Exchange involved a wide array of products, including stocks[131], bonds[132], call/put options, futures and forward contracts, and (since 1640) repos (Gelderblom and Jonker, 2004). In addition, it also pioneered fractional trading (more on this in the next chapter) with ducatons, each of which represented 1/10th of an ordinary Dutch East India Company share. Launched in 1683 to facilitate public participation in equity trading (as the company's shares had risen by far in

---

[129] See De la Vega (1957, 21, para 204); in addition, Vega paints a very rudimentary picture of trade-execution:
"A member of the Exchange opens his hand and another takes it, and thus sells a number of shares at a fixed price, which is confirmed by a second handshake. With a new handshake a further item is offered, and then there follows a bid." (De la Vega, 1957, 21, para 208).

[130] The formation of investment clubs at the time was largely motivated as a means of reducing the risk of moral hazard and adverse selection in trading. To that end, these clubs aimed at attracting individuals of reputation for honesty in their dealings, as well as financial capacity (Petram, 2014). This fostered intra-club trading (club-members felt safer trading among themselves) and deterred adverse behaviour (it would imply expulsion from the club–and further negative reputational externalities). As Mosselaar (2018) noted, most trading ended up being conducted within such clubs by 1670.

[131] The only two stocks traded during Vega's time were those of the Dutch East India Company and the Dutch West India Company (*Geoctrooieerde Westindische Compagnie*). Established in 1621, the latter was primarily involved in Dutch trade (including slave trade) in the Caribbean and West Africa. Although it was granted a monopoly in Atlantic trade, by 1638 this monopoly was reduced to specific activities (including slave-trade, arms-trafficking, and Brazil-wood; see Trivellato, 2017, 153). Despite a promising start, its fortunes largely dwindled following the loss of Dutch Brazil in the 1650s and by 1674 it had to be restructured (as its shares had lost almost all their value). Its successor company was launched afterwards to continue primarily with slave trade, yet documenting rather modest performance (reflected also in the lower dividends paid, compared to the Dutch East India Company). See De la Vega, 1957, 19-20, para 194-195.

[132] Both government bonds, as well as Dutch East India Company bonds.

price)[133], they ended up amplifying speculation by both large investors and small traders.[134] Key facets (which Vega often notes and which will further be discussed in the next chapter) of the Amsterdam Stock Exchange include the strong presence of small investors, as well as manipulative schemes, thus suggesting a significant role for noise trading (which would help explain the high volatility characterising stock prices in the market).

Much of the trading focused on price-differences (i.e., it was speculative), while there existed three settlement modes (instant[135]; monthly[136]; prolongated[137]) of transactions. Speculators relied largely on leverage and short-selling (at least since 1609), the latter being a paradox, since it was legally proscribed. In general, contracts involving future delivery of a stock were deemed illegal; a series of decrees[138] first issued by Frederick Henry (Netherlands' *Stadtholder*)[139] in 1610 enabled a trader party to such a contract to (as the expression is cited in De la Vega, 1957)

---

[133] "With average daily wages around 0.9 guilders (Hart, 1997, 33) and the price of shares at over 15,000 guilders it would have taken a laborer's entire life earnings to purchase one full share."–Stringham (2003, 333).

[134] The settlement of ducaton-trades was fixed to take place on the 1st day of each month and involved the participation of a General Cashier, who would enter all orders in a book (charging each order's parties a very small fee for his services). On the 1st day of each month, at 13:30, two exchange members would inform the General Cashier of the price of Dutch East India Company's ordinary share; the General Cashier then would specify the ducaton-value and the transactions would then be settled. The 1688-crisis ultimately led to the demise of the ducaton-market.

[135] Instant settlement involved the seller depositing his shares with the Bank of Amsterdam and the buyer depositing the corresponding purchase amount, followed by a confirmation of the deal by the Bank.

[136] Monthly settlement of accounts was undertaken with the mediation of rescounters and involved delivery of shares on the 20th day of the month, with payment on the 25th.

[137] Prolongated settlement involved a time bargain for the settlement; the involved brokers issued two copies of a contract form (with terms and conditions of the trade including names, dates, and prices), which the two parties filled out, signed and exchanged. Once the settlement was formalised by the rescounter, the forms were re-exchanged by the signatories (De la Vega, 1957, 24, para 227).

[138] The first decree was issued on February 27th, 1610; further decrees were issued in 1621 (when the 12-year Truce terminated), 1623, 1624, 1630, 1636, and 1677. See Stringham (2003).

[139] The *Stadtholder* in the Netherlands of the time was the highest executive official (in effect, Governor) of the country, appointed by the provincial assemblies ("states") governing the seceded Dutch provinces following their rebellion against the Spanish Crown in the late 16th century.

"appeal to Frederick", and render the contract void. In Vega's words, according to those decrees:

> "[…] he who sold shares for future delivery without putting them on the time account should be exposed to the danger (because he has sold something he does not own) that the buyer will not take the pieces at the time fixed upon." (De la Vega, 1957, 6, para 29).

The ban pertained to naked short selling (known as *windhandel*–"wind trade"–in the Netherlands at the time; De Marchi and Harrison, 1994), namely selling shares for future delivery, while maintaining an empty account in the company's share register (i.e., selling stocks one did not own); however, borrowing a share from a shareholder and selling it on the market was allowed. To put the decrees banning short-selling into context, we need to recall Lemaire's bear-raid on Dutch East India Company shares in 1609, in the aftermath of Matelieff's recommendations; following company directors' lobbying to the States General to tackle bearish speculators, the Dutch State responded with the first decree of 1610. Despite the series of decrees issued, it appears that anti short-selling regulation was never really enforced (and was finally repealed in January 1689); this may be partly attributed to the lack of a uniform financial regulatory framework[140]–and perhaps also to the costs involved in the ban's enforcement (see the discussion in Stringham, 2003, 329).

2.5 Joseph de la Vega

Joseph[141] de la Vega (full name: Joseph Penso de la Vega Passarinho Félix) was the second-born child of Isaac Penso Félix (1608-1683) and Esther de la Vega (d. 1679), both Sephardi former *conversos* from the Iberian Peninsula. His father originally lived in Espejo, a small town near Cordoba in Andalusia (Southern Spain). Following a prison stint with the Inquisition, he migrated to Middelburg (in the Netherlands), and then in Antwerp, before settling down for a short spell in Hamburg. While in Hamburg, Isaac Penso served as *parnas* in the city's *ma'amad* (in 1655) and married Esther de la Vega and had his first four children born. By 1656 he moved his family to Amsterdam, entering the banking business. Isaac Penso was a major community donor and vehement advocate of religious education within his community; he held religious meetings at home, while

---

140 The repeal of the anti short-selling regulation coincided with the initial introduction of regulation of trading in the Amsterdam Stock Exchange (Stringham, 2003, 329).
141 Vega often spelled his first name as "Josseph", or "José" (Davidi, 2019a).

also participating in the establishment of a Talmudic academy (De la Vega, 1957).[142] Several of his children (all four of his sons and a daughter) married members of the Sephardi family of Alvares Vega from Antwerp (De la Vega, 1957).[143]

Joseph de la Vega was born in Hamburg in 1650 and moved to Amsterdam with his family in 1656. Educated at the *Ets Haim* school in Amsterdam, he was originally earmarked to join the local rabbinate. Nevertheless, he seems to have opted for a life of trade and travel, frequenting several European cities with a potent Sephardi presence (Antwerp; Hamburg; Livorno[144]), before settling down in Amsterdam in 1683, following his father's passing. His return saw him shifting his attention to stock trading, while at the same time devoting ample time to writing. Vega passed on November 13th, 1692.[145]

Vega held senior roles at several literary academies of his community in Amsterdam[146] and produced a series of writings of various types and genres, including marriage poems, poems dedicated to royalty, novels, allegories in rhymed prose (*maqama*), speeches, and moral/philosophical books (see Davidi 2019a; b). In 1667, when he was only 17, he composed a drama in Hebrew, titled *"Asirei ha Tikva"* (*"Prisoners of Hope"*), which was warmly welcomed by Amsterdam's Sephardi community; as Davidi (2019a) mentions, its paratext stretched around 40 pages containing praises by community paragons. First printed in Amsterdam in 1673 and in Livorno in 1771, it the first written *and* published *auto sacramental*[147] work in Hebrew, as well as the first Hebrew-language theatrical piece to be printed *and*

---

[142] As per Davidi (2019b), Isaac Penso's name appears regularly since 1665 in the list of the Sephardi community's taxpayers; this suggests that he maintained a financial standing allowing him to play a leading role in his community (possibly as *parnas*, similar to his position in Hamburg).

[143] Isaac Penso's children (in order of birth) were: Sara (b. 1645), Joseph (b. 1650), David (b. 1654), Jochebet (b. 1655), Abraham (b. 1656), Rafael (b. 1659), Ribca (b. 1662), Abigail (b. 1663), and Lea (b. 1664).

[144] Livorno (also known as Leghorn) in the 17th century was the centre of the coral industry (dominated by the local Jewish community; Heertje, 2015), as well as a centre of Jewish printing for N. Africa at the time (Davidi, 2019a).

[145] Aside from knowing his wife's name (Raquel Alvares Vega), we have no information as per his descendants.

[146] *Academia de los Sitibundos* and *Academia de los Floridos*; both were established by Isaac Nunez ("Manuel") Belmonte (one of the Amsterdam *ma'amad's parnassim*) in 1676 and 1685, respectively (with meetings of both academies held at his home).

[147] The *auto sacramental* genre involved a dialectic between the representatives of good and evil, while fighting over control of the human soul (for a detailed discussion of said genre, see Davidi, 2019a).

distributed.[148] After his return to Amsterdam in 1683, Vega published a series of other works (probably composed during his overseas years), including "*Rumbos peligrosos*" ("*Dangerous Paths*"), a collection of short novels. By 1688, he published "*Confusion de Confusiones*" ("*Confusion of Confusions*"–our book's focus), while by 1692 he published a collection of twelve rewritings of biblical stories (Davidi, 2019b).

2.6 *Confusion of Confusions*

The first edition of *Confusion of Confusions* appears to have been released sometime around the first half of 1688; on its front cover, Vega included a dedication (dated 24th of May, 1688) to Duarte Nunez da Costa.[149] All in all, the book offers some technical explanations of a number of aspects of stock exchange operations for the first time (that we know of) in financial history; in his book, Vega details a rather sophisticated (for the standards of its time) market with cash and derivatives operations. Vega's language could be described as flowery, as it combines a discussion of financial concepts and descriptions of how the Amsterdam exchange operated, with moral/philosophical contemplations and recourse to Biblical/Classical elements. The book was originally written in Spanish and it is likely that it was intended as a manual for speculators from the Sephardi community in the-then nascent domain of equity trading. Kellenbenz (De la Vega, 1957) speculated that it might have been written for Vega's brothers who lived in London (David and Rafael), or other Sephardi in London who were eager to engage in equity trading.[150] As Kellenbenz further states:

> "The author stressed in the preface to his book that he had three motives in writing the dialogues: first, his own pleasure; again, for those who were not active in the trade, he desired to describe a business which was on the whole the most honest and most useful of all that existed at that time; and, lastly, he wished to describe accurately and fully the tricks that rascals knew how to employ in that business." (De la Vega, 1957, xi)

The manuscript's completion largely coincided with the turbulent 1687-1688 years, when the market crashed ahead of the Dutch *Stadtholder*

---

[148] See Davidi (2019a, 199-200) for a detailed discussion of its significance in (and influence on) Hebrew-language literature of its time.

[149] The patriarch of one of the leading families in the Sephardi community; see Nogueira (2002; 2017).

[150] Cardoso (2002) speculates that its target-audience was Amsterdam's Sephardi community.

William III's invasion of England, an invasion which culminated into what came to be known as the Glorious Revolution. The collapse had intensified by August 1688, when rumours of an impending war led to massive ducaton sales (in effect terminating the ducaton market), leading to a market crash in Amsterdam. The rumours were largely motivated by the naval preparations that William III was undertaking; by September 5th of that year, it had become clear that William III was going to invade England and that France was going to declare a war in support of the English incumbent King James II and VII. The materialisation of the invasion led to massive purchases of Dutch East India Company shares, as a show of faith in William's endeavour, which culminated in the Company's shares skyrocketing by year-end (Davidi, 2019b).[151]

The book probably enjoyed limited attention; limited circulation might have been one factor (Cardoso, 2002).[152] Either way, the book began gaining in awareness when the German economist Richard Ehrenberg mentioned it in his essay "*Die Amsterdame Aktienspekulation im 17. Jarhhundert*" ("*The Amsterdam Stock Speculation in the 17th Century*") published in the 1892 *Jahrbücher für Nationalökonomie und Statistik* (*The Journal for Economics and Statistics*). Eventually, the book was translated into German (1919), Dutch (1939) and English (1957), with the latter involving the translation from the original in Spanish only of those sections directly relevant to the stock exchange.

More formally, the book entails no strict order in its flow, with topics examined intermittently, drawing on a mix of trading technicalities, moral/ethical reflections, recourse to the Bible, as well as Greek and Roman history/mythology. The book is structured in four dialogues with three actors, the Shareholder (who stands in for Vega), the Merchant, and the Philosopher. The Merchant and the Philosopher have heard about/witnessed share-trading before, yet know little about it and are hesitant to participate; to that end, they resort to the Shareholder for enlightenment on the issue. The Shareholder, in turn, explains to them how trading is conducted, what types of transactions exist and how fraud works in trading. Following this, they both engage in trading shares of the Dutch East India Company — yet with little success.

---

151 A perhaps less advertised aspect of that crisis was its impact on the reputation of the Sephardi community in Amsterdam at the time; as Trivellato (2017, 144) mentions "In 1688, community leaders forbade congregants from dealing in stocks in the vicinity of the Portuguese synagogue in order to fend off accusations that Jewish brokers had caused the financial crash of the Amsterdam stock market."

152 The original Spanish edition has survived in only a limited number of copies; see Cardoso (2002) and Davidi (2019b).

In the first dialogue, the Shareholder debates the moral fabric of equity trading and defines the term "share". He then introduces the Dutch East India Company and its dividend policy, before embarking on a typology of its main investor-clienteles: the large capitalists ("princes"), who are long-term investors focusing on dividend-income; the merchants, who are interested in hedging their risks; and the speculators ("gamblers"), who profit from price-differences. He also discusses the role of the Bank of Amsterdam; persons offering leverage with equity as collateral (hypothecation of stocks); brokers; and "rescounters" (persons in charge of settling transactions). He also offers definitions and applications of options and details as per their settlement.

The second dialogue focuses on the volatility of share prices and its determinants and offers some advice on investments. It showcases variations in the behaviour of buyers and sellers, and how their opinions diverge given their heterogeneity in news-interpretation (with news often being false and made-up). It further offers a description of the Bulls' and Bears' syndicates, their features and interactions.

The third dialogue focuses on contracts used in price-negotiations among trading participants and the settlement procedures utilised for cash and derivatives' purchases. It then introduces the Dutch West India Company, discusses how investors performed pair-trading between shares of the Dutch West India and Dutch East India companies and then discusses the market for ducatons. Finally, the fourth dialogue focuses on speculative aspects of trading, elaborates on various manipulative schemes of the Bulls and Bears, discusses broker-ethics and offers a description of the 1688-crisis.

Overall, the book reflects the Baroque style, which was in vogue in the 17th century; said style combined a pessimism in secular view with a nostalgia for return to the harmonious (more compatible with religion) medieval order of affairs. Its genre involved finding the truth via a series of riddles and hidden clues ("masks"), reflections, duplications, and mirrors. Amid such contrasts, it strived to provide moral interpretation of things in light of their divine origin and hidden spiritual meaning (which was assumed to have been forgotten during the 17th century). Vega's book showcases these contrasts via an allegorical transfiguration of the reality of the stock market. Drawing on the context of a very uncertain environment (stock market), where a spirit of *homo homini lupus* is described to prevail, people avail themselves of every opportunity, adapting to changing circumstances, in order to chase the "myth" of "quick profit". At the book's climax, the 1688-crisis debunks that myth, marking a moment of truth and providing a cathartic experience to those involved in the hypnotic chase of stock profits.[153]

2.7 Concluding remarks

This chapter has offered an extensive discussion of several aspects of the background underlying *Confusion of Confusions*. The chapter has introduced the history of Vega's Sephardi community, how many of them ended up in Amsterdam, as well as the organisation of their community in the Dutch capital. It has further delineated the evolution of Amsterdam's Stock Exchange since the world's first initial public offering of the Dutch East India Company there. Finally, it has provided a short biography of Vega himself, alongside an overview of the structure and style of *Confusion of Confusions*. As mentioned above, Vega's book provides ample descriptions of investors' trading practices–and behaviour; to that end, the next chapter will focus on the analysis of *Confusion of Confusions* on the premises of the behavioural finance paradigm. To perform this analysis, we shall rely on the 1957-translation by Kellenbenz, the sole English-language translation of the book known to date.[154] On very few occasions, we will also draw on Corzo et al. (2014), whose paper discusses a very limited number of quotes from Vega's book from a behavioural finance angle, drawing on the Spanish original; some of these quotes appear also in the Kellenbenz-translation (De la Vega, 1957), while others do not–and it is the latter that we further include in our discussion in the next chapter.

---

[153] For a detailed discussion of the Baroque style of the book, see Davidi (2019b).

[154] Throughout this book, any references of text from *Confusion of Confusions* based on Kellenbenz's translation will be noted using the following convention: (De la Vega, 1957, page/s number/s, paragraph/s number/s).

CHAPTER 3

CONFUSION OF CONFUSIONS: A BEHAVIOURAL FINANCE ANALYSIS

This chapter provides a critical assessment of Vega's work from the perspective of the behavioural finance paradigm. As will be demonstrated, a series of biases and heuristics (and associated trading patterns) that contemporary behavioural finance research has documented over the past four decades, were first identified and discussed in his book over 330 years ago.

Before we begin, the reader is reminded that the institution of the organised stock exchange was, in and of itself, an innovation in the 17th century; similarly innovative was the concept of the joint stock trading company (for which the stock exchange provided a secondary market for its shares), first pioneered by the Dutch East India Company during Vega's time. Innovations represent novel opportunities with little-known prospects surrounded by a positive general outlook, thus representing a mix of an uncertain promise with optimistic ignorance. In such cases, fundamentals' analysis becomes harder (fundamentals may either not be available or be surrounded by ambiguity), thus leaving investors with little choice but to resort to non-fundamentals (such as rumours and sentiment) to inform their trades. In view of this, people are more likely to invest in the innovation due to speculation (i.e., to profit by trading on it), rather than because of its earnings' prospects (Kindleberger and Aliber, 2005)[155], thus enhancing the potential for noise trading (and the temptation of preying on it). Such conditions (enhanced ambiguity; noise trader risk) were clearly evident in the 17th century Amsterdam stock market (as Vega amply demonstrates) and would be, thus expected to have culminated in a rather complex and risk-laden trading environment.

As mentioned in Chapter 1, when people are faced with complexity, they are more likely to resort to biases and heuristics to tackle it. This chapter

[155] People may also invest in innovations driven by faith in their (unknown, but imagined) prospects, a faith which connects the object of investment with humans' unconscious desires (see the discussion in Tafler, 2018 for more on this).

discusses how this applied to 17th century Dutch investors, by presenting (in alphabetical order) their biases/heuristics (and associated trading patterns), as reflected in the text of *Confusion of Confusions*. For each of those biases/heuristics, the relevant quote/s from the Kellenbenz-translation of Vega's text[156] are presented, before showcasing how the bias/heuristic (or associated trading pattern) is related to the market's context of the time. We will also draw on the knowledge regarding this bias/heuristic (or associated trading pattern) from behavioural finance research to assess how its presence in the text compares to this research (e.g., in terms of definition or motivations) and how it is explained via the latter.

3.1 Biases, heuristics and behavioural trading patterns in Vega's work

3.1.1 Attention-grabbing effect

Humans possess limitations in their attention (see the discussion in Nekrasov et al., 2023), an issue that is further amplified in today's signal-rich world, whereby multiple stimuli compete for our attention. As a result, attention to some tasks has to be prioritised and attention to some tasks sacrificed, thus suggesting that investors will not utilise all available information. The relevance of this to investment decisions has been explored in the literature (Odean, 1999; Barber and Odean, 2008), which has confirmed the role of attention in facilitating (primarily less sophisticated) investors' decisions, particularly on the buy-side. This is justified via the fact that the buying decision constitutes a far more onerous task (it involves choosing from among the universe of publicly listed stocks), compared to the selling one (which involves choosing from among the stocks one already holds in their portfolio). Attention-grabbing buying can therefore amplify noise trading, and motivate rising levels of volume and volatility (Ding and Hou, 2015; Andrei and Hasler, 2015; Dzieliński et al., 2018). A series of attention-grabbing proxies have been proposed to date; examples include abnormal returns (e.g., Barber and Odean, 2008), abnormal volume (e.g., Gervais et al., 2001), media releases (e.g., Tetlock, 2007) and internet activity indicators (such as Google Trends; see e.g.,

[156] The Kellenbenz-translation pertains to De la Vega (1957) and will often be used to denote the latter. As mentioned in the previous chapter, on very few occasions, we draw on Corzo et al. (2014), whose paper discusses a very limited number of quotes from Vega's book from a behavioural finance angle, drawing on the Spanish original. Whereas some of these quotes appear also in De la Vega (1957), others do not–and it is the latter we also include in our discussion in this chapter.

Dzieliński et al., 2018), to mention but a few. Although the issue of attention in the context of stock-picking in Vega's time may seem far less obvious (after all, equity trading revolved around only two stocks–Dutch East India Company and Dutch West India Company), evidence from his book suggests that attention-grabbing was relevant to manipulative schemes; more specifically:

> "Secondly, a broker in whom the [bear] syndicate has confidence is given the order to buy secretly a batch of shares from an [avowed] bull, without revealing his real principal. But he sells the very same shares with a good deal of publicity, while it is shouted out that even the bulls are making sales. As the broker wants to sell to one bull the same shares he has bought from another bull, the first one sees that the story about the sales of the latter is true. Alarmed, the second bull sells his shares also. Seized by fear, everybody tries to forestall the sales of the others and regards any advice to buy as deceitful." (De la Vega, 1957, 31, para 293)

> "Ninthly, the [bear] syndicate encourages a friend whose judgment is esteemed, whose connections are respected, and who has never dealt in shares, to sell one or two lots of stock while the risk of loss is borne by the group. The notion [lying behind this manoeuvre] is the belief that anything new attracts attention, and that therefore the decision of this person [to sell stocks] will produce astonishment and will have important consequences." (De la Vega, 1957, 32, para 293)

The first excerpt above denotes how manipulators invoked investors' attention by creating noise around a true event. A broker (presumably from the Bears' syndicate) buys shares from a bull (i.e., a member of the Bulls' syndicate) with the purpose of selling them to another bull, alongside making a public statement of their source–namely that a bull sold them to him. Clearly this was engineered to convince bulls that, since a member of their own was selling, there must have been some serious reason for it (given bulls' aversion to selling) and they should be selling too. The second excerpt involves no public statement. Rather, a respectable figure of Amsterdam society is nudged by members of the Bears' syndicate to sell a batch of stocks on their account, in order to attract the attention of other investors–and presumably nudge them, in turn, to sell as well.[157]

---

[157] The opinions of influential individuals in Dutch society could impact investment decisions in 17th century Amsterdam Stock Exchange; this was perhaps due to the Dutch East India Company (and its West India counterpart) being under the oversight of the States General (see previous chapter), suggesting that the opinions of key figures in the Dutch government were far from indifferent to the investment public. As Vega further mentions: "Despite all these absurdities, this confusion, this

The above denote that attention-grabbing did affect investors' decisions in Amsterdam's stock market–thus providing seminal evidence on the role of attention-grabbing in equity trading. As Vega shows, it proved important in cases of manipulative intent, motivating higher trading interest by investors–and therefore higher volume (and, potentially, volatility), in line with the predictions of the behavioural finance literature. Contrary to the latter, however, the examples that Vega provides show attention-grabbing to motivate investors' sales (rather than purchases). There are two things to note here: first, Vega's examples hail from Bears' manipulative schemes (where attention-grabbing was necessary for the success of Bears' endeavours to depress stock prices); second, as mentioned earlier, with only two traded stocks on the stock exchange, the role of attention-grabbing on the buy-side would be expected to be far less important (compared to modern-day markets). Furthermore, it is worth noting that the attention-grabbing tools mentioned in these two excerpts are not uncommon nowadays. In the first excerpt, Bears relied on negative publicity (to hurt the Bulls), something very similar to modern-day media releases (Tetlock, 2007); in the second excerpt, Bears utilised an important social figure to motivate sales, something (again) very similar to the impact of contemporary opinion leaders' trades/views on market prices (Sul et al., 2017; Ajjoub and Zhao, 2020; Ante, 2020; Leung et al., 2022).

3.1.2 Cognitive dissonance

Cognitive dissonance refers to the feeling of discomfort an individual experiences when a) faced with information that challenges his own beliefs, b) engages in an action that is unpleasant, yet also beneficial for him, or c) says or does something at odds with his beliefs (see Harmon-Jones and Mills, 2019 for a review of the literature). The impact of cognitive dissonance on investments has been empirically confirmed in several contexts, including mutual fund investors' recollection of funds' performance (Goetzmann and Peles, 1997), the performance of trading strategies (Antoniou et al., 2013), the realisation of losses from delegated versus non-delegated investments (Chang et al., 2015) and the presence of anomalies (Altanlar et al., 2018). Vega alludes to the notion of cognitive dissonance in the following:

---

madness, these doubts and uncertainties of profit, means are not lacking to recognize what political or business opinions are held by persons of influence. He who makes it his business to watch these things conscientiously, without blind passion and irritating stubbornness, will hit upon the right thing innumerable times, though not always." (De la Vega, 1957, 11-12, para 79)

> "But what surpasses all these enormities . . . and what is hardly believable (because it seems to be complete fancy rather than over-exaggeration) is the fact that the speculator fights his own good sense, struggles against his own will, counteracts his own hope, acts against his own comfort, and is at odds with his own decisions. . . . There are many occasions in which every speculator seems to have two bodies so that astonished observers see a human being fighting himself. If, for example, there arrives a piece of news which would induce the speculator to buy, while the atmosphere prevailing at the stock exchange forces him to sell, his reasoning fights his own good reasons. At one moment his reasoning drives him to buy, because of the information that has just arrived; at the other it induces him to sell because of the trend at the Exchange." (De la Vega, 1957, 22, para 208)

In the above, Vega offers us the first known reference in equity trading history to investors' cognitive dissonance, articulated in a fashion clear enough to render it comparable to modern-day practice. The speculator here is assumed to be in two minds, as his own analysis dictates a purchase, while the market's trend/sentiment prompts him to sell. The ensuing cognitive dissonance is perhaps the result of the highly speculative nature of the 17th century Amsterdam Stock Exchange, with its rampant noise trading and volatility. Even if the speculator's analysis were correct, sudden shifts in sentiment could render its predictions futile. Rationally choosing making money over proving his own analysis correct, it would not be surprising to witness him discard his own research, choosing to ride the market trend instead. The dilemma of Vega's fictitious speculator is consonant to similar dilemmas faced by modern-day rational investors; in the face of outperforming noise (i.e., non-fundamental) strategies, evidence (Lux, 1998; Chiarella et al., 2014; He and Zheng, 2016; Frijns and Zwinkels, 2020) suggests that fundamentals-driven investors are likely to deviate from their pattern and adopt those strategies.

3.1.3 Divergence of opinion/trader-disagreement

Trader-disagreement involves investors interpreting information in different ways. This may occur, if investors exhibit differences in their mode of information-processing, use different valuation models (or the same model in different ways), or simply because their confidence in their information (or information-processing skills) varies with time. As Carlin et al. (2014) note in their discussion of the literature on the subject, disagreement can reflect heterogeneity in beliefs (which are, however, subject to updating), or–in the extreme–persistent divergence of opinion. To the extent that opinions need not be based on fundamentals, it is not necessary that a higher disagreement level is associated with more informed or rational trading[158]; it does, however, imply a greater participation of investors and, to that end, has been found to occur during periods of higher volatility and volume. Whether the interaction of disagreeing investors can foster learning among them remains an open issue. Investors can rationally update their beliefs (in which case, the divergence in their beliefs may begin to decline; Geanakoplos and Polemarchakis, 1982); equally, however, their learning may be hampered, due to behavioural biases (such as overconfidence; Menkhoff and Nikiforov, 2009)[159], or persistence in their divergence of opinions (Carlin et al., 2014).

Vega offers the following quotes relevant to trader-disagreement:

> "In order that you should not come to the conclusion that the movements of the stock exchange are inexplicable and that nothing is firm, take note and realize that there are three causes of a rise in the prices on the exchange and three of a fall: the conditions in India, European politics, and opinion on the stock exchange itself. For this last reason the news [as such] is often of little value, since counteracting forces [may] operate in the opposite direction." (De la Vega, 1957, 9, para 65)

> "[…] one portion of the speculators would buy on the strength of the Indian news, while another sells on the basis of the unclear European situation." (De la Vega, 1957, 9, para 66)

> "For example, it seems] incompatible with philosophy that the bears should sell after the reason for their sales has ceased to exist, since the philosophers teach that when the cause ceases, the effect ceases also. But if the bears obstinately go on selling, there is an effect even after the cause had disappeared. Moreover, while philosophy teaches that different effects are ascribable to different causes, ... at the stock exchange some buy and some sell on the basis of a given piece of news, so that here one cause has different effects." (De la Vega, 1957, 15, para 100)

---

[158] On the dichotomy between "private information" and "opinion", see the discussion in De Long et al. (1990b, 735-736); *e contrario*, see Cookson et al. (2022), who find that higher trader-disagreement implies stronger informed trading.

[159] An investor who is overconfident and attributes his gains (losses) to his skill (bad luck) is unlikely to update his beliefs via newly incoming information (or process that information in an unbiased fashion). A very relevant bias here is the confirmation bias (Hart et al., 2009), according to which people overweight (underweight) information that confirms (disconfirms) their prior views. By definition, confirmation bias violates Bayesian updating of beliefs; although with more information coming in, we should update accordingly, confirmation bias makes us focus only on information that we agree with. This can boost overconfidence, leading us to ignore things we do not want to know about–in effect, hampering our learning.

> "[...] some speculators consider a certain piece of news favorable, others unfavorable. Facts are changed by emotions, and they appear to each person in a different light." (De la Vega, 1957, 15, para 100)

The quotes from paragraph 65 denote that investors' opinions of the news coming from India or Europe was even more important than the news itself, since people interpreted it in different ways ("counteracting forces [may] operate in the opposite direction"). As paragraph 66 outlines, people diverged in their trades when faced with contradictory signals, implying that uncertainty amplified disagreement in the market.[160] Paragraph 100 is even clearer about this, as it states that "at the stock exchange some buy and some sell on the basis of a given piece of news", while "some speculators consider a certain piece of news favorable, others unfavorable". In addition, the "But if the bears obstinately go on selling, there is an effect even after the cause had disappeared" indicates the presence of persistence in investors' opinions- a persistence that presumably fostered overreaction and trending in prices (see sub-section 3.1.9 for more on this).

How relevant are the above to modern behavioural finance? Carlin et al. (2014) show that higher disagreement is associated with higher volume and volatility–both of which are also associated with noise trading (see the discussion in Chapter 1) and typified the Amsterdam Stock Exchange of the time. In such a highly speculative environment it is very much likely that investors traded on their own personal opinions, which may or may not have been founded; in a market, where fundamental information was so opaque[161] and rumours abounded, they, admittedly, had little choice. The interaction of those opinions in the trading process boosted the Dutch market's volume and volatility, thus further amplifying noise in the market. As a result, the evidence on trader-disagreement furnished by *Confusion of Confusions* is in line with what behavioural finance research outlined over three centuries after the book's compilation.

3.1.4 Herding

In paragraph 67, Vega mentions the following:

---

[160] The fact that signals are contradictory also implies some level of cognitive dissonance.

[161] The reader is reminded here about the ill-transparent accounting disclosure practices of the Dutch East India Company (see Chapter 2), as well as the long delays in Company-specific news' transmission from its overseas trading posts (that, effectively, led such news to become obsolete).

> "Merchant: In this chaos of opinions, which one is the most prudent?
> Shareholder: To go in the direction of the waves and not fight against the powerful currents." (para 67)[162]

In paragraph 289, Vega begins to describe the techniques bearish traders used to corner the market. He mentions that bears begin by placing sales orders for future execution ("time sales"), which motivate the anticipated slump in prices in the future. In his words:

> "They [the ring of the bears] strike the first blow with time sales, reserving the cash sales for the moment of greater distress. They sell 50,000 pounds for various [forward] months, an operation through which a decline of prices is bound to occur. The declining tendency spreads, the [ring of the] bears receives help from other speculators, and it becomes obvious that, with so broad a participation, the object [of the machinations] is sure to be achieved. [...] As there are so many people who cannot wait to follow the prevailing trend of opinion, I am not surprised that a small group becomes an army. [Most people] think only of doing what the others do and of following their examples." (De la Vega, 1957, 30, para 289).

The above clearly allude to imitative behaviour (herding), whereby investors suppress their beliefs in favour of the consensus (which is what paragraph 67 mentions), irrespective of what their private signals or fundamentals dictate (Hwang and Salmon, 2004). Herding, by definition, involves similarity in behaviour following interactive observation (Hirshleifer and Teoh, 2003), something not too hard in the case of the Amsterdam market in the 1680s, given the small population of investors involved.[163] We have no evidence as to who was herding behind whom; in paragraph 79 (which we mentioned earlier), Vega mentions:

> "Despite all these absurdities, this confusion, this madness, these doubts and uncertainties of profit, means are not lacking to recognize what political or business opinions are held by persons of influence. He who makes it his business to watch these things conscientiously, without blind passion and irritating stubbornness, will hit upon the right thing innumerable times, though not always" (De la Vega, 1957, 11-12, para 79).

[162] The excerpt from this paragraph does not exist in the Kellenbenz-translation; it is referenced here from Corzo et al. (2014), who drew on the original Spanish edition of *Confusion of Confusions*.

[163] The IPO of the Dutch East India Company involved just over 1,100 investors from the Amsterdam-chamber alone (which contributed around half the IPO's proceeds, with the other half contributed by the rest five chambers–see Chapter 2).

This suggests that there existed influential figures in Dutch society whose views impacted on investors' decisions (something which we discussed in section 3.1.1 earlier); in many cases, however, much of this "influence" reflected rumour-mongering via Bulls'/Bears' manipulative schemes (as much of the *Fourth Dialogue* reveals).[164] What Vega describes in paragraph 289 is herding on the sell-side, in view of the downturn initiated by the Bears; in this case, other investors would choose to unload their positions, in order to curtail their losses (or simply due to believing the market-wide selling to signify adverse prospects for the Dutch East India Company). This panic selling, likely coupled with investors' generalised aversion towards risk/losses, motivated sell-herding.[165]

There exists no singular motive for herding, with research suggesting a dichotomy of herding into intentional and spurious (e.g., Holmes et al., 2013). Intentional herding occurs when there exists an actual or perceived asymmetry in the market; for example, investors less informed or skilled than others would be expected to mimic their better informed/skilled peers in order to benefit in their trades (Devenow and Welch, 1996).[166] Spurious herding, on the other hand, involves similar responses to commonly observed signals, without interactive observation being necessary. For example, people herd spuriously when employing the same trading strategy (style investing; see e.g., Barberis and Shleifer, 2003), draw on similar information sets (investigative herding; see e.g., Hirshleifer et al., 1994), are under the influence of similar behavioural biases (e.g., Barber et al., 2009), or project commonalities in their professional background and framework (e.g., Teh and DeBondt, 1997).

So, what drove herding among 17th century Dutch investors? A lot of evidence in Vega's narrative suggests that investors herded behind the trades of those they believed to be informed (irrespective of whether their information was genuine or not). As shall further be discussed in the sub-

---

164 See also the following relevant excerpt from the original Spanish edition of *Confusion of Confusions* (cited by Corzo et al., 2014 and not included in the Kellenbenz-translation): "There are times in which the powerful investor is followed by many, even at the cost of losing money." (para 73)

165 Correlated panic-selling motivated by loss/risk-aversion during market slumps is a very common observation in equities markets; see, e.g., Shi et al. (2011) and Elkind et al. (2022).

166 Research suggests two different types of benefits: informational ("I follow those more informed than me") and professional (lower-skilled fund managers track the trades of their better-quality peers, in order to improve their career prospects; by imitating the trades of better-skilled fund managers, they thus aim to come across as better-skilled themselves). For more on this, see the discussion in Kallinterakis and Gregoriou (2017).

sections on manipulation, much of the *Fourth Dialogue* in his book outlines a series of manipulation tactics aimed at getting investors to believe that manipulators possessed valuable information–and chase their trades. As a result, investors were keen to herd to extract informational payoffs from their (actually or supposedly) more informed peers (who often aimed at preying on them)-*ergo*, their herding was intentional. Specifically, regarding brokers, those with lower skills (or connections in the market) may also have been tempted to track the trades of their better-able (or -connected) peers, in order to enhance their reputation in the market–thus further denoting intentional herding on their part.

However, spurious herding was also a viable possibility; as we have also mentioned thus far (and will do so later on, too), investors projected several behavioural biases and it is possible that the commonality of those biases motivated them to reveal similarities in their trades. The expected commonality in risk/loss-aversion that prompted panic-selling in paragraph 289 is one such example; what is more, what Vega mentions in paragraph 67 (that it is more prudent to follow the trend, rather than go against it) further implies the presence of conformity bias (see the discussion in Hirshleifer, 2001), which, if widespread, would be expected to amplify investors' herding. Investigative herding was also relevant; in the event that investors traded on similar news-signals (whether genuine or fabricated), this could also boost herding in the market. The above, therefore, suggest that investors in 17th century's Amsterdam stock market projected herding tendencies for reasons very similar to those of contemporary investors, denoting that herding is one of the oldest and most permeating expressions of investors' behaviour in capital markets.[167] The fact that stock trading back then was a nascent innovation raises interesting implications regarding herding among investors in modern-day innovative instruments or newly emerging sectors.[168]

---

[167] For narrative evidence of investors' herding in pre 20th century markets, see Mackay (1841) and Galbraith (1994). Academic research on herding in such markets has been notably scarce; evidence on this has only been documented for the Berlin stock exchange (1920-1923) by Bohl et al. (2012) and the St Petersburg stock exchange (1865-1914) by Gavriilidis and Kallinterakis (2023). For more on the widespread presence of herding in contemporary markets for various asset classes, see Kallinterakis and Gregoriou (2017).

[168] For more on herding in newly emerging asset classes or sectors, see the discussion in Andrikopoulos et al. (2021) and Economou et al. (2023). The fact that Amsterdam hosted the first-ever organised secondary equity market must certainly have motivated herding *toward equity trading* (i.e., Dutch individuals to mimic those of their fellow citizens who had decided to invest in equities), aside from herding *in*

3.1.5 Information-based manipulation

Information-based manipulation (also known as "pump and dump"; Allen and Gale, 1992; Van Bommel, 2003; Putninš, 2012) refers to cases whereby an individual (or a group of individuals) attempts to intentionally influence the price of a stock to their benefit by disseminating false news to the market.[169] The ultimate aim here is to motivate investors' interest in order to trigger a sharp move (primarily, a rally) in the price of a stock–and, once this happens, sell first and pocket the profit. Companies more likely to fall prey to such schemes are relatively small and unknown ones (e.g., start-ups or penny stocks), which have so far attracted little attention/are little known. The higher uncertainty surrounding such companies helps render any rumours circulated about them more believable–or harder to fact-check.[170] In the case of the Amsterdam Stock Exchange in the 1600s, such practices were very common; unlike modern-day markets with a large number of listed stocks, these practices were confined to short-run price-movements in the Dutch East India Company and Dutch West India Company stocks.[171] Below we cite a series of relevant excerpts from Vega's book (all from the *Fourth Dialogue*):

> "Thirdly, the syndicate of the bears sells some blocks of shares for cash to one of the wealthy people who live on the hypothecation of stocks. As it is known that the latter [as a matter of course] sell at once for future delivery the shares which they have bought for cash, the syndicate bids its broker [charged with the execution of the manoeuvre], before the fixing of the prices [of the day], to send a message very secretly to the agent of every business firm [represented on the Exchange], a communication which will soon be an open secret, to the effect that the great capitalist has received important news, and that alarmed by it he intends to sell stocks. When afterwards the sales are actually made, the swindle seems to be verified, the

equity trading (which implies investors peer-mimicking in their trades), in order to experiment with a novel investment option for their funds.

[169] These rumours may be circulated via the press, financial analysts, or brokers.

[170] A small stock is easier to corner as well due to its smaller free-float, compared to a large one. Information-based manipulation need not focus exclusively on already listed companies; it is also possible that manipulators can foster the initial public offering of a very small company in order to benefit from the investors' interest their rumours will stimulate. In general, the owner of the targeted company is most likely party to the manipulation underway, either through tacit price-support (e.g., not selling his shares) or by pleading ignorance to the scheme.

[171] The lower trading activity enjoyed for the most part by the Dutch West India Company stock suggests that such schemes were likely applied for stocks of the Dutch East India Company.

aim is reached, fear spreads, and a crash of prices is brought about." (De la Vega, 1957, 31, para 293)

"The eighth trick [of the syndicate of the bears] is the following: if it is of importance to spread a piece of news which has been invented by the speculators themselves, they have a letter written and [arrange to have] the letter dropped as if by chance at the right spot. The finder believes himself to possess a treasure, whereas he has really received a letter of Uriah which will lead him into ruin. On his own initiative, he makes known the contents of the letter to his coterie and points out the reasons which will move the syndicate to sell when it receives news of this kind. And if a storm breaks out on the Exchange that very day, the news seems thus to be confirmed, the suspicion ratified, and the apprehensions explained." (De la Vega, 1957, 32, para 293)

"The tenth trick [of the syndicate] is to whisper into the ear of an intimate friend (but loud enough to be heard by those who lie in wait for it) that he should sell if he wants to make money. . . . "The stones speak," says the prophet, and "the walls have ears," says the proverb; and our conspirators know this truth to be verified by experience. If their secret spreads, their advice [seems to have met] with approval, and [when] it becomes obvious that they sell blocks of stock, the walls and the stones do [appear] to talk; people seek the secret reasons of the [whispered] assertions; one is grateful for the hint; and, as cheating a close friend is thought impossible, the manoeuvre meets with success, the fish take the bait, the net becomes filled, the victory is celebrated, and the intention of the ring is very advantageously achieved." (De la Vega, 1957, 32-33, para 304)

"When a cunning broker [interested in a price rise] has to buy two thousand pounds [worth of shares], he first buys but one thousand pounds [worth] in order to convey the impression that he will take [stocks worth] at least twenty [thousand] pounds. As soon as he sees that another [broker] buys too, whether to follow his example or to flatter him, he approaches the latter and talks to him in a hushed voice expressing anguish (but audibly enough to be heard by those who make efforts to catch his remarks). He implores the other for Heaven's sake not to ruin him and not to influence the prices, for he has still to take care of a tremendous volume, and if there were a disturbance the transaction would be a failure, and a loss in evitable. Now the Exchange takes as a serious endeavor what is only a ruse. Immediately everyone begins to buy in order to secure the profit which, according to the [presumed] tendency, is to be expected." (De la Vega, 1957, 37-38, para 333)

In the above excerpts, manipulators introduced rumours to the market in different guises: rumours regarding the anticipated trades of wealthy investors; rumours printed on a letter left for others to find; rumours on sales-timing; and rumours of a fictitious buying interest of huge proportions.

Though Vega admits that such schemes were not always crowned with success, they were widely practiced. The popularity of such schemes hinged largely on the noisy informational environment of the Dutch market at the time. Fundamentals were either unknown or hard to assert (and sometimes–given the lack of communication technology–were known with a delay, thus being superseded by other information). On the other hand, investors were not sophisticated and had limited to no investment experience/knowledge (considering that equity trading was an innovation of the time and they were trading in the world's first-ever organised stock exchange). Their behavioural biases and heuristics further nudged (at least some of) them to fall prey to such schemes, often leading to temporary price-swings (via overreacting to rumours) and sentiment-shifts in the market, as we shall discuss in later sub-sections of this chapter.

As a result, information-based manipulation in Vega's time was fostered as strongly by informational uncertainty/noise as in modern-day stock markets; the only difference pertained to its regulatory treatment. Whereas the 20th century witnessed the introduction of regulatory crackdowns on manipulative practices (see e.g., Allen and Gale, 1992; Putninš, 2020), Amsterdam's stock market in the 17th century was largely self-regulated, entailing no such regulatory provisions. Investors seeking trust in trading had to resort to personal/kinship connections or networks (e.g., via membership in investment clubs) to identify trustworthy counterparts in their transactions on the stock market (Petram, 2014).

3.1.6 Limits to arbitrage

The pricing of the Dutch East India Company's stock reflected deviations from the law of one price, which would-as per neoclassical finance predictions-be expected to motivate arbitrage. More specifically:

> "The possibility of quick sales increases the value of the stocks in such a manner that the shares of the Amsterdam chamber command a higher price than those of all other chambers. This happens only because speculation does not exist at the other places in these Provinces. The dividends, apart from small expenses, are the same for the outside chambers; yet the shares of the chamber of Zeeland are quoted 150 per cent, of Enkhuysen 80 per cent, of Hoorn 75 per cent, of Rotterdam 30 per cent, of Delft 70 per cent less than the shares of the Amsterdam chamber." (De la Vega, 1957, 13-14, para 93)

Furthermore, with respect to ducaton-trading:

> "The reason why nearly all of the [speculators] participate so eagerly in the trading in small shares is the intention of the buyers of large shares to sell them as small ones, (because at the beginning of the month the price of the small shares is higher than that of the large ones). [...] He who has bought large shares and sold ducaton shares, makes efforts to have the stick kept low [i.e., the trading continued a few minutes] in order to reap the profit from the small shares, and to continue his engagements in the large shares. He, however, who has bought ducaton shares because he has sold large shares [short], demands the stick to be lifted up, in order to secure his profit, and will await the conclusion of his business with the large shares, hoping for yet a greater profit." (De la Vega, 1957, 27-28, para 239)

How do the above link to arbitrage–and limits to it–from the modern behavioural finance literature? As mentioned in Chapter 1, arbitrage is rendered costlier/riskier in view of real-world factors (fundamental risk; implementation costs; horizon risk; synchronisation risk; noise trader risk; model risk), several of which are mentioned outright (or implicitly) by Vega here. Let us begin with the first quote (paragraph 93), which reveals several interesting things. First, Dutch East India Company shares traded at different prices across chambers, thus *prima facie* reflecting an inefficiency (in the modern sense of the term, i.e., as a violation of the efficient market hypothesis) *per se*. This inefficiency was predicated on the fact that one and the same stock was priced differently in each chamber, even though its fundamental value was the same across all six chambers (dividends were the same for all chambers).[172] Second, the higher pricing at the Amsterdam chamber was ascribed by Vega to speculation due to the higher volume that this chamber enjoyed. The fact that Vega treats high volume as a causal factor of the Amsterdam chamber's observed price-premium is further interesting, as it provides the first historical evidence on the high-volume premium in equity markets; according to this, any shocks in trading volume boost a stock's visibility in the market, culminating in enhanced traders' interest–and hence, higher prices.[173]

---

[172] Since the same share traded at six different prices, it would be impossible for investors to know which price was the correct one (from a fundamental valuation standpoint). The irregularity of dividends, in terms of payment frequency and nature (they were often paid in kind) further contributed to this uncertainty as per the stock's accurate valuation.

[173] For more on the high-volume equity premium, see Merton (1987), Gervais et al. (2001), Kaniel et al. (2012), Bali et al. (2014), Wang (2021) and Israeli et al. (2022). It is also worth noting here that the high-volume equity premium is relevant to attention-grabbing effects, since an abnormally high volume, by definition, constitutes an attention-grabbing proxy (see the discussion in section 3.1.1).

Paragraph 93 also offers some real-world factors of the time that introduced limits to arbitrage. Key in the latter were implementation costs; since shares were non-transferable across chambers, this introduced institutional frictions in their trading;[174] additional issues were raised by liquidity risk (even if transferability were possible, the lower volume of the other five chambers would have rendered arbitrage potentially more costly) and brokerage fees (to which Vega often refers in-text).[175] Noise trader risk further rendered arbitrage harder; as Amsterdam's prices were always higher due to the higher speculation/volume of the Amsterdam chamber, this suggests that trading on that chamber was unlikely to have been motivated by fundamentals (an indirect allusion to the contemporary argument that noise trading boosts the volume of trade; Black, 1986).

The violation of the law of one price was further observed in ducaton-trading; with a ducaton amounting to a tenth of a share, it stands to reason that it should be worth a tenth of a share's value. In other words, ducaton-prices would be expected to obey a 1:10 parity with the prices of the Dutch East India Company's share; in reality, however, ducaton-pricing appeared to have been decoupled from that of ordinary shares, with each ducaton being valued at more than 10% of the share's price. Why this was the case is not directly clear from Vega's text; Kellenbenz (De la Vega, 1957, 27) argues that this may have been due to the fact that the settlement date of ducatons was the 1st day of the month, while it was the 20th of each month for shares. This delayed price discovery for shares versus ducatons would suggest that one could use ducatons to finance share purchases with some confidence (given the systematic overpricing of ducatons). As a result, the above implied the presence of another anomaly in the modern sense of the term (violation of the 1:10 parity) that persisted for several years (from 1683 when ducatons were introduced, until 1688, when ducaton-trading was officially suspended). This, however, leaves an unresolved issue: why were ducatons systematically overpriced versus ordinary shares? Part of the explanation may lie with the fact that ducatons were more exposed to trades by small investors, whose speculative activity led ducatons to be priced over

---

[174] Although one cannot preclude the existence of ways to circumvent this limitation, we are not aware of evidence indicative of this. From an arbitrage viewpoint (and absent this limitation), one could go long on the "cheap" shares of the Dutch East India Company (from the other five chambers) and short on the "expensive" share of the Dutch East India Company (from the Amsterdam chamber); alternatively, one could perform arbitrage among the shares of the other non-Amsterdam chambers (since the stock traded at different prices across them).

[175] Brokerage fees amounted to 3 gulden per stock traded (De la Vega, 1957, 20, para 195).

and above ordinary shares.[176] Larger traders probably took little issue with that, since ducaton-overpricing allowed them to speculate on shares with lower risk:

> "Shareholder: Some clerks have discovered that the speculation in ordinary shares (which are called large or paid-up shares) was too hazardous for their slight resources. They began, therefore, a less daring game in which they dealt in small shares. For while with whole shares one could win or lose 30 gulden of Bank money for every point that the price rose or fell, with the small shares one risked only a ducaton [3 gulden] for each point." (De la Vega, 1957, 26, para 238)

Could arbitrage have been utilised to restore the 1:10 parity? Vega does not mention such aspirations among traders and, perhaps for good reason. Since ducatons allowed large traders to speculate on shares with lower risk, any departure from this parity was welcome–more so, because it was predictable in direction (ducatons were always overpriced). Second, for arbitrage to be practiced, it would have taken many large traders to coordinate their trades; although such coordination was far from uncommon, Vega shows (as we will discuss in the next sub-sections) that this mainly involved manipulative intent, not arbitrage.[177]

As a result, the secondary market for the Dutch East India Company shares presented two peculiar inefficiencies: the company's share lacked a single value (its value varied across the six chambers) and the one-tenth fractions of that share (the ducatons) were priced at more than 10% of the share's value. Although arbitraging such inefficiencies would prove tempting nowadays, this was prevented back then by a series of real-world

[176] This overpricing refers to ducatons being priced at over 10% of the value of an ordinary Dutch East India Company share (thus violating the 1:10 parity), not that they were priced more than ordinary shares themselves.

[177] The departure from the 1:10 parity was only one reflection of inefficiency in the 17th century Dutch market; it is not entirely clear whether ducatons were traded only in the Amsterdam chamber or in the other five chambers as well. Given the lower speculation levels of the latter (see the earlier discussion on paragraph 93's excerpt), it is likely that the 1:10 parity may have been obeyed more closely there (though that would raise an issue of ducatons themselves trading at different prices across chambers–similar to ordinary shares–and, hence another inefficiency!). On a more general note, arbitrage was probably not feasible either way, since there was no universally acceptable fundamental valuation of the Dutch East India Company shares. Even if arbitrageurs could enforce the 1:10 parity in the market, that would still not imply efficient pricing, as there was no objective way to establish that ordinary shares themselves were efficiently priced.

factors equally relevant to introducing limits to arbitrage in contemporary markets.

3.1.7 Noise trading

The concept of noise trading implies trading on anything but information (Black, 1986). As a result, noise traders are likely to be of low relative sophistication, in terms of both information (which is likely to either be lacking or of dubious quality) and its processing (which is likely to be mediated by biases/heuristics). This suggests that noise traders are prone to misvaluing assets and their activity can give rise to inefficient prices. To the extent that their trades make the market more liquid, this helps informed investors trade more comfortably on their information; nevertheless, noise traders impound noise into prices, leading them to project departures from fundamental valuations (see e.g., Shiller, 1981).

Vega offers several hints on the presence of traders of such profile in the stock exchange of his era; more specifically:

> "The fourth principle: Whoever wishes to win in this game must have patience and money, since the values are so little constant and the rumors so little founded on truth." (De la Vega, 1957, 10, para 74)

> "They will sell without knowing the motive; they will buy without reason. They will find what is right and will err without [merit or] fault of their own." (De la Vega, 1957, 10, para 74)

> "Moreover, it is foolish to think that you can withdraw from the Exchange after you have tasted [the sweetness of the honey]. . . . He who has [once] entered the [charmed] circle of the Exchange is in eternal agitation and sits in a prison, the key of which lies in the ocean and the bars of which are never opened" (De la Vega, 1957, 18, para 159)

The above quotes indicate that the Amsterdam Stock Exchange was largely susceptible to noise trading; the prevalence of rumours, alongside the broad participation of unsophisticated individual traders almost guaranteed that prices would entail noise and volatility in their formation process (see also the sub-section on overreaction).[178] How much these

[178] The following excerpts from the original Spanish edition of *Confusion of Confusions* (cited by Corzo et al., 2014 and not included in the Kellenbenz-translation) further denote the noise in pricing in the Amsterdam market at the time:

traders viewed trading as a form of gambling is exemplified by what is mentioned in paragraphs 74 (whereby it is stated that they buy or sell for no apparent reason) and 159 (where it is implied that trading had become some sort of addiction for many of them). As a result, the above confirm the modern behavioural finance literature (e.g., Dorn et al., 2008; Barber et al., 2009; Sicherman et al., 2015) on individual investors being natural candidates for noise trading. Much of the latter is predicated on similarities in retail investors' behavioural biases, which often translate into higher correlations in their trades; as we discuss elsewhere in this chapter, phenomena such as overreaction and herding were very widespread in the Dutch market of the time.

The presence of noise traders must have been even more intense in ducaton-trading, where the lower stakes involved would naturally have attracted less sophisticated investors. Vega confirms this as follows:

> "This branch of trade has been increasing during the last five years to such an extent (and mainly with a certain group which is as boisterous as it is quick-witted) that it is engaged in by both sexes, old men, women, and children. . . . Therefore, the means devised to reduce hazards has in fact made the dangers more widespread. The speculation has been so extended that one deals in whole regiments of [ducaton] shares, as if they were matches, and I fear that some day those concerned in the business will be burnt and ruined. [...] When a mirror is broken, each piece of crystal remains a mirror, the only difference being that the small mirrors reflect one's countenance in miniature and the large ones in larger size. . . . Stock shares are similar to mirrors, at least a special sort of mirror which makes it appear that the reflected object is hanging in mid-air, or that sort that makes the viewers stiffen from amazement because, while they are looking, they see themselves flying by. [...] Fearful persons broke this mirror [the large "East" shares] and cut the crystal into pieces by agreeing to regard each 500 pounds of the large shares as 5,000 small ones. They intended thereby to moderate the trade, but they managed merely to make many transactions out of one, and from one mirror many. [...] The pleasure in this gamble has grown to such an extent that people who cannot gamble a ducaton per point risk a stuiver, and those to whom a stuiver is too much, risk a still smaller coin. Even children who hardly know the world and at best own a little pocket money agree that each point by which the large shares rise or fall will mean

---

"According to the news, the shares should be quoted at 1000, but the actual value is only 500; however, the shares should be quoted at 400, but it happens that they are quoted much more highly." (para 71)
"Therefore, it is not important that the basic value of the shares be practically nothing as long as there are other people willing to close their eyes and support those contradictions." (para 81)

> a certain amount of their pocket money for their small shares. ... If one were to lead a stranger through the streets of Amsterdam and ask him where he was, he would answer, "Among speculators," for there is no corner [in the city] where one does not talk shares." (De la Vega, 1957, 27-28, para 239)

As ducatons were byproducts of original shares' splits (each ducaton represented one-tenth of a share), they come somewhat close to what modern finance terminology would term "stock split" (though clearly a split in ten, not in half). What is remarkable is that Vega's description of ducaton-trading raises issues very similar to those of modern-day stock-splits. As research (Kamara and Koski, 2001; Angel et al., 2004; Chen and Wu, 2009) has shown, stock splits lead to an increase in small trades (i.e., enhanced trading by small investors), coupled with a rise in volatility. This is largely due to the fact that the lower price post-split renders it easier for small investors to purchase the stock; in addition, owing to the nominal price illusion (Birru and Wang, 2016), individual investors view low-priced stocks as more likely to rise in price and, hence are more eager to speculate on them (e.g., the case with lottery stocks). However, more than stock-splits, ducatons come closer to the notion of fractional trading; being the subject of limited research to date (Da et al., 2021; Bartlett et al., 2022; Tripathi and Rengifo, 2023), fractional trading involves investors buying as little as $1 of large corporations' stocks, whose individual share valuations may be large (and, hence, prohibitive for the modest financial means of the average retail investor). Again here, evidence suggests that the introduction of fractional trading has amplified the potential for noise trading (via fostering retail investors' participation; Tripathi and Rengifo, 2023), alongside volatility (Bartlett et al., 2022) and bubble-formation (Da et al., 2021)–similar to ducatons in Vega's time.

As a result, noise trading was widely present in the world's first organised stock exchange; 17th century Dutch noise traders appear notably similar to modern-day noise traders in terms of their sophistication, speculative intent and impact over volume and volatility. As this chapter also demonstrates in several sub-sections (especially those pertaining to non-fundamental speculation and manipulation types), they also appear remarkably similar in terms of their status as prey to speculators and manipulative schemes (Leuz et al., 2023).

3.1.8 Non-fundamental speculation

In the absence of fundamental information, some investors choose to rely on information pertaining to some aspect of the (current or predicted) trading activity; this is known as non-fundamental speculation and, in effect, constitutes a noise-based strategy. Examples of aspects of the trading activity that non-fundamental speculators often focus on include the order-flow (Madrigal, 1996), technical indicators (De Long et al., 1990b)[179], and inside information on trading activity (such as the front-running of clients by their own brokers; Khwaja and Mian, 2005). Vega offers a series of references to such behaviour:

> "Despite all these absurdities, this confusion, this madness, these doubts and uncertainties of profit, means are not lacking to recognize what political or business opinions are held by persons of influence. He who makes it his business to watch these things conscientiously, without blind passion and irritating stubbornness, will hit upon the right thing innumerable times, though not always." (De la Vega, 1957, 11-12, para 79)

This paragraph refers to investors using opinion-leaders' views as inputs for their trading decisions. Modern-day opinion-leaders do, indeed, command following in capital markets and there are people who do trade on their published views, as research suggests (Sul et al., 2017; Ajjoub and Zhao, 2020; Ante, 2020; Leung et al., 2022). Such inputs are clearly not of a fundamental nature, yet motivate a following wide enough to permit price-impact across various asset classes.

> "The brokers who intend to seek quick gains through price changes, i.e, by getting large orders from their customers and speculating extensively [on their own account] in executing these orders, experience the same fate. For, although it is not their intention to keep the shares [bought for their clients] for any length of time at their own risk, they cannot foresee incidents that may occur suddenly during this time [while they are holding the shares]. [...] In order to gain from [the second] of the three methods mentioned above, the brokers must be popular at the stock exchange, for if, at the conclusion of the business, they are asked about their customers, they need the help of a good friend who will sign the contracts for them and will conceal the true character of the affair." (De la Vega, 1957, 28-29, para 239)

> "A broker, for example, receives an order to sell 20 shares; if a broker for the bulls receives the order, he begins to perspire from fear and to rage with fury, for, if he sells first the shares bought on his own account, he fears that it will become known and that he will be accused [of sharp practice]. If he keeps his own shares and carries out the sale as ordered, he fears a slump in consequence of the sales so that he could dispose of his own shares only at

[179] "An alternative rational investment strategy would be to gather information about future noise trader demand shifts and to trade in anticipation of such shifts. Such information can come from examining trading volume, price patterns, buy/sell ratios, and other "chartist" indicators." (De Long et al., 1990b, 727).

> a great loss. […] The broker in question was doing business on his own account because he expected a rich profit. If [in such a situation] he gets an order, the carrying-out of which binds him in a direction contrary to his own transactions, […] [he] sells his own shares secretly. He tries to kill the snake around a man's neck without hurting the man; he seeks to avoid the damage [to his own interests] without acting harmfully as far as the specific order is concerned" (De la Vega, 1957, 34, para 305)

> "When a bull enters such a coffee-house during the Exchange hours, he is asked the price of the shares by the people present. He adds one to two per cent to the price of the day and he produces a notebook in which he pretends to put down orders. The desire to buy shares increases; and this enhances also the apprehension that there may be a further rise (for on this point we are all alike: when the prices rise, we think that they fly up high and, when they have risen high, that they will run away from us). Therefore, purchase orders are given to the cunning broker. But, in order slyly to reach his own objectives, he replies that he has so many other orders that he cannot be at anyone else's disposal. The naive questioner believes in the sincerity of the statement; his desire to buy becomes even more ardent; and he gives an unrestricted order to another broker. As soon as this becomes known to the sly [first] fellow, the latter hurries to the Exchange and offers the shares at more than the day's price. The other broker, previously uninterested, buys at the higher price because he believes there to be new reasons making for the change in the price and enhancing the desire for investment. At times the increase in the price is maintained, deception has been crowned with success, and what seemed originally as madness comes to have the appearance of cleverness." (De la Vega, 1957, 35, para 322)

> "I am more surprised that already for a long time some enterprising brokers have run [two establishments], one for true brokerage and another for Exchange transactions on their own accounts. At the delivery of the stocks they have designated themselves as principals, and promoted the idea that a change in the name meant an actual change." (De la Vega, 1957, 37, para 333)

The above excerpts refer to brokers who speculated in the market having prior knowledge of their client's orders; in this case, they made efforts to conceal this in order not to be exposed (see the discussion in paragraphs 239 and 305). Paragraph 322 reveals a more elaborate form of speculation; whereas the broker has taken down purchase orders from his clients, he then tacitly incites other investors to place purchase orders with other brokers. Once the price has risen high enough after this, he then offers to sell at that price, thus pocketing a profit.[180] Paragraph 333, however, raises an even more elaborate pattern of broker-behaviour: apparently some brokers operated one brokerage for their clients and one for proprietary trading. Under such conditions, they aimed at front-running their clients who had submitted their orders to the first brokerage by trading (presumably ahead of those orders' execution) via the second brokerage. As a result, brokers in Vega's time engaged in front-running and predatory trading against their clients in remarkably similar ways to their modern-day peers (see e.g., Khwaja and Mian, 2005).[181]

It is hardly surprising that non-fundamental speculation held sway in the Dutch market of the 1600s. Fundamental information was hard to come by (or assert); as mentioned earlier, news often took a long time to arrive (and when it did, it may well have been obsolete), while the pricing of shares did not subscribe to market efficiency (as discussed in the sub-section on limits to arbitrage). Considering that the bulk of the investors' population was far from sophisticated in investment knowledge terms, resorting to non-fundamental information was a logical choice for many of them. What is more, the legal framework for penalising adverse practices (such as front-running) of the time was not developed enough to deter such behaviour, thus rendering it tempting for many brokers to adopt such practices.

3.1.9 Overreaction and Underreaction

Overreaction (underreaction) relates to investors reacting excessively (with a delay) to news.[182] If investors overreact to news that is positive (negative), they become over-optimistic (-pessimistic), bidding the stock's price up (down) more than the news' content suggested in the first place. If investors underreact, then the news will be incorporated into prices gradually,

---

[180] This is a non-fundamental speculative strategy of a rather hybrid nature, as it involves front-running (broker takes the opposite position from his clients), coupled with direct and indirect ramping (he both enters clients' orders at successively higher prices and also incites others to do so via other brokers).

[181] Such practices were known as "card-sharping" back then, as Kellenbenz elaborates in his translation; see also Vega's following quote: "[…] this business has necessarily been converted into a game, and merchants [concerned in it] have become speculators. Had the conversion of these merchants into speculators been the only change, the harm would have been bearable, but, what is worse, a portion of the stock brokers have become card-sharpers and, though they are familiar with the blossoms, they nevertheless lose the fruits." (De la Vega, 1957, 5, para 18).

[182] For more on over- and underreaction, see DeBondt and Thaler (1985; 1987), Jegadeesh and Titman (1993) and the excellent review by Galariotis (2014).

with a given delay. Clearly, both forms of reaction violate market efficiency. As far as overreaction is concerned, it has been attributed to the representativeness heuristic (see e.g., Barberis and Thaler, 2003), which motivates people to overweigh recent events and downweigh base rate information. If this holds, prices will record excessive upward/downward movements (leading to over/underpricing), which eventually will be corrected, hence leading to return-reversals (which would imply return-predictability). Both over/underpricing and return-predictability run counter to market efficiency (see Chapter 1); what is more, return-reversals can further amplify volatility (e.g., So and Wang, 2014) and entail a clear destabilising potential for securities' pricing. As per underreaction, it has been ascribed to a series of behavioural biases (e.g., conservatism; anchoring)[183] and can lead information to be incorporated into prices with a delay (again running against market efficiency).

Confusion of Confusions contains a host of relevant references pertaining to both concepts; as regards overreaction, examples include the following excerpts:

> "Sometimes a quiet state of prices is obtained and the Exchange is influenced by neither favorable nor unfavorable news. . . . Suddenly a cloud appears which portends a storm. The sellers of shares rejoice and start talk about the uncertainties in the situation and the possibilities of disasters." (De la Vega, 1957, 11, para 79)

> "One has to pay attention to the different tides and to trim one's sails according to the wind. Formerly twenty speculators ruled the exchange and as the smallest circumstance had an influence, the shares fell 30 per cent because of an apprehension and 50 per cent because of a letter." (De la Vega, 1957, 13, para 90)

> "The fall of prices need not have a limit, and there are also unlimited possibilities for the rise." (De la Vega, 1957, 14, para 93)

> "The expectation of an event creates a much deeper impression upon the exchange than the event itself. When large dividends or rich imports are expected, shares will rise in price; but if the expectation becomes a reality, the shares often fall; for the joy over the favorable development and the jubilation over a lucky chance have abated in the meantime." (De la Vega, 1957, 14, para 94)

> "[I would also remark that] a twenty per cent drop in the stock prices is not large enough to be considered a serious blow. . . . You do not have to despair

[183] See e.g., Barberis et al. (1998) and Hung et al. (2022).

> and to bemoan your fate, for, as the price may drop twenty per cent overnight, it may also rise fifty per cent in the same period." (De la Vega, 1957, 18, para 159)
> "For example, it seems] incompatible with philosophy that the bears should sell after the reason for their sales has ceased to exist, since the philosophers teach that when the cause ceases, the effect ceases also. But if the bears obstinately go on selling, there is an effect even after the cause had disappeared." (De la Vega, 1957, 15, para 100)

> "Numerous [brokers] are inexhaustible in inventing [involved manoeuvres], but for just this reason do not achieve their purposes. The bulls spread a thousand rumors about the stocks, of which one would be enough to force up the prices. A thousand stratagems of the Contremine are launched in an effort to cause ill-temper on the exchange. If by chance, however, some of the fabrications come to be confirmed, the real situation may turn out to be of less consequence [than one might anticipate]. If it becomes known, for instance, that a situation is not as favorable[184] as one feared, the prices rise in spite of a deterioration of the situation. On the other hand, a decline [of values may] set in when a propitious event falls short of expectations." (De la Vega, 1957, 37, para 333)

> "And, that you may see that a revival of the stock exchange has already been brought about, I draw your attention to the fact that the shares which had gone down by 180 per cent because of the apprehension of an outbreak of the war have risen again by 100 per cent [of the face value] since its declaration." (De la Vega, 1957, 41, para 358)

The above denote that news (actual or fabricated by manipulators) prompted overreaction on behalf of Dutch investors (see e.g., the quotes from paragraphs 79 and 100), producing wild swings in the price-formation process. Indeed, the quotes from paragraphs 90, 93, 159 and 358 clearly illustrate the hugely volatile nature of prices when responding to news.[185] The quotes from paragraphs 94 and 333 point toward the reversals following the overreaction; investors overreacted to news, but this overreaction did not continue up to the point when the announced event materialised. A possible explanation for this is that the market had already discounted the

---

[184] Although the Kellenbenz-translation reads "favorable", the sentence probably makes better sense, if this were to read "unfavorable" (since it is unlikely one would fear a favourable situation).

[185] Although one would be tempted to classify this volatility as "excess" (in the spirit of Shiller, 1981), this would probably be inaccurate; volatility is termed "excess" when controlling for fundamentals and, as we discussed earlier with regards to limits to arbitrage, the fundamentals of the Dutch East India Company were far from unambiguous for investors.

news upon its announcement, hence the realisation of the announced event was not informative any more (this is suggested in paragraph 94).[186] Another possible explanation is that, if reality proved to be more (less) positive compared to what the original news had implied, this could have led prices to exhibit reversals–something implied in paragraph 333.[187]

The 1688-crisis is discussed by Vega in the *Fourth Dialogue* and its narrative (paragraphs 354-358) reveals the intermittent presence of both over- and underreaction during the crisis' unfolding; we will present the crisis' narrative summarised as follows. 1688 bore a promising outlook for the Dutch economy, with not even the bears speculating for a market slump. Some initial reports of a few Dutch East India Company ships facing delays in their voyages did not shift the overall optimistic sentiment (*ergo*, investors underreacted to those reports). Once the ships, however, arrived with merchandise from India, it appeared that the merchandise amounted to 34 (as opposed to previous year's 50) tons of cargo. This time, this proved enough to trigger a price-collapse, with investors engaging in massive panic-selling (i.e., they overreacted to the news). Soon thereafter, however, fresh news arrived, stating that, due to higher commodity prices, selling those 34 tons would fetch an amount of money equal to that from the sale of previous year's 50 tons. Despite its positive content, investors underreacted to the news, persisting with their sales-momentum, more so since the bears proclaimed the impending outbreak of a war. As mentioned

---

[186] In a rather perverse way (given the opacity of fundamentals and dominance of noise traders in the market), the possibility of the market discounting the news seems to suggest an element of efficiency; of course, much of the news seemed to reflect rumours–and discounting those would certainly not contribute to the market's efficiency. An alternative interpretation of this possibility hinges on the realities of the time; given the absence of modern (i.e., 21st century) communication technologies in the 17th century, any piece of news could take months to be transmitted, by which time other developments of completely antithetical content to that piece of news may have arisen (thus rendering the original news obsolete). Vega proposes this possibility in paragraph 66, where he states that:

"[…] an untoward event occurring subsequent to the acquisition of the news, but before the conclusion of the business [by the Company] may destroy this splendor and contentment". (De la Vega, 1957, 9, para 66)

[187] In this case, the reversal would have occurred, if an announced positive (negative) event proved to be less positive (negative) than anticipated. This would be similar to the initial overreaction, followed by a reversal in view of earnings' surprises in modern-day capital markets; see, for example, the discussion in Alwathnani et al. (2017). Of course, if the announced positive (negative) event proved to be more positive (negative) than anticipated, that would be expected to foster persistence in overreaction.

in Chapter 2, the bears' foresight proved correct; indeed, the anticipated invasion of England by the Dutch *Stadtholder* William III (which motivated the Glorious Revolution) did take place later that year, with its successful conclusion ensuing in massive purchases of Dutch East India Company shares-and prices catapulting to their highest levels ever in the stock's price-history (Davidi 2019a).

In all fairness, however, one must admit that the lack of objectively defined fundamental valuations of stocks in Vega's time rendered over- and underreaction to news far from surprising. The opacity surrounding the Dutch East India Company's financials and the wealth of rumours on circulation rendered it almost impossible for investors to generate a proportionate response to news; the fact that most investors bore little to no investment knowledge/experience (with many of them probably viewing trading as a gambling activity of sorts) further removed the potential for rational news-processing. As a result, over- and underreaction were rife in 17th century Amsterdam's Stock Exchange, thus confirming the latter as being a rather inefficient, noise- and volatility-prone market (not unlike many modern-day ones) and constituting the first known reference of such phenomena in the history of equity markets.

3.1.10 Prospect theory

In Chapter 1, we discussed how prospect theory offers a more realistic depiction of decision-making, compared to expected utility theory. In brief, prospect theory postulates that people are risk-averse in the domain of gains, risk-seeking in the domain of losses, and that losses hurt more than equal-sized gains please. Although prospect theory lags behind expected utility theory in terms of inception[188], elements of prospect theory are apparent enough in Vega's book. More specifically:

> "When a loss occurs, the losers are expected to pay at least what they have available at the moment, and it might be expected that, as the wound is fresh, there would be no new injury. But though the proverb "He who once is intoxicated. . ." condemns such goings-on, emotion has greater power than the warning of proverbs; gullibility and seduction cannot in any way be prevented." (De la Vega, 1957, 6, para 34)

In this paragraph, Vega presents the case of people who have lost in their investments and who, as a result, would be expected to refrain from

---

188 Whereas prospect theory was coined in the late 1970s, elements of expected utility theory were first proposed by Bernoulli in the early 18th century.

investing; however, this is not happening and they continue to trade. This suggests risk-seeking when losing, in line with the predictions of prospect theory. Whether this risk-seeking is motivated by the need to recover one's losses or due to trading having become an addiction is not clear here; it does, however, cast doubt on whether there was a learning effect from trading.[189] In the next paragraphs, Vega turns to what an investor should do when winning:

> "The second principle: Take every gain without showing remorse about missed profits, because an eel may escape sooner than you think. It is wise to enjoy that which is possible without hoping for the continuance of a favorable conjuncture and the persistence of good luck." (De la Vega, 1957, 10, para 66)

> "The third principle: Profits on the exchange are the treasures of goblins. At one time they may be carbuncle stones, then coals, then diamonds, then flint-stones, then morning dew, then tears." (De la Vega, 1957, 10, para 66)

What Vega explicitly advises here is that gains should be realised, without waiting for them to grow in size; given the volatility of the Dutch market of his time, his advice makes intuitive sense. As a result, this is a direct allusion to prospect theory's risk-aversion in the domain of gains–namely, that gains are realised more quickly than losses (or else, that winning stocks are sold more quickly than losing ones). This has also come to be known as "disposition effect" and has been extensively studied–and confirmed–for a variety of markets internationally.[190]

---

[189] With Dutch investors being eager to trade even after they had lost, this likely resembles gambling motives. Such behaviour suggests they were unlikely to have traded on information (something not completely unjustified, considering the prevalence of rumours and opaque fundamentals in 17th century Amsterdam's Stock Exchange), thus not rationally updating their beliefs. Interestingly enough, reinforcement learning appears also not to be informing their trades: whereas an individual with a negative investment experience would be presumed to refrain from (or, at least moderate) his investment activities, they, nevertheless, continued to trade even in the face of losses.

[190] See the surveys by Pleßner (2017) and Gutiérrez-Nieto et al. (2023). See also the following relevant excerpts from the original Spanish edition of *Confusion of Confusions* (cited by Corzo et al., 2014 and not included in the Kellenbenz-translation):

"A wise man eats right away the fruits found in season without any delay." (para 97)

"It is wise to collect some profit without waiting to collect all profit. Profits can be compared to arrows and it is wise to collect the profit of each arrow." (para 127)

> "One has to pay attention to the different tides and to trim one's sails according to the wind. Formerly twenty speculators ruled the exchange and as the smallest circumstance had an influence, the shares fell 30 per cent because of an apprehension and 50 per cent because of a letter. Today there are as many speculators as merchants (for those playing the game merely for the sake of entertainment and not because of greediness are easily to be distinguished), and they have had sad experiences through unjustified fears. For this reason everyone watches his stocks like a jewel, and they find it extremely painful when a real loss occurs. But fearing a mere menace means to experience grief and sorrow twice, and in advance of reality." (De la Vega, 1957, 13, para 90)

This paragraph combines several behavioural concepts; *prima facie*, it refers to loss-aversion, since losses hurt more (than equal-sized gains please) in prospect theory. However, Vega's lines here reveal something more subtle. The "everyone watches his stock as a jewel" suggests that people view the shares under their possession extremely proprietarily, possibly watching their price-changes frequently enough. This is reflective of several behavioural forces. First, it implies the presence of the endowment effect (Kahneman et al., 1990), according to which people value more what they have (compared to what they do not) and demand a higher price to accept parting from it. Loss-aversion can motivate such preferences–which can also be driven by the affective response to losing something that we possess (Hirshleifer, 2015). Relevant to the latter, Vega mentions "But fearing a mere menace means to experience grief and sorrow twice, and in advance of reality." Essentially, what he implies here is being afraid of losses before they occur; this denotes anticipated emotions (Lucey and Dowling, 2005), namely emotions expected to be experienced given a certain outcome (in this case, losses). The implied anticipated emotion in the case of losses in investing is regret–which again helps explain why investors prefer to hold onto their losses, rather than realise them: before you realise your losses, you entertain the hope of a reversal; once you realise them, regret comes to the fore.[191]

"Miracles should not be expected from the stock exchange and the only ones who will be happy will be the ones who enjoy the initial successes." (para 128)

[191] This could be a regret for buying stocks that made you lose–or a regret for selling them while they were losing and did not wait for a rebound in their price. Either way, realising your losses confers negative utility to you, as per realisation utility theory (Barberis and Xiong, 2012). This theory further helps explain why (as per prospect theory and disposition effect) investors sell their winners more quickly: this is because selling a winner confers positive utility to you (in the form of a positive investment experience and elevated self-esteem). See also the following relevant

Second, it suggests the possibility of myopic loss-aversion (Benartzi and Thaler, 1995), according to which, the more frequently you monitor the performance of your investments, the riskier they appear. It is easy to see how the endowment effect is related to myopic loss-aversion: the more proprietary one feels about his holdings, the more likely one is to check on their performance frequently–and the more frequently this happens, the more likely one is to witness their prices exhibit upward/downward swings. This would naturally be expected to make one's investments appear riskier, and lead one to believe that it is more likely to experience a loss from them (which, if true, would lead him to experience regret). The fact that prices were so volatile in Vega's time only helped amplify Dutch investors' susceptibility to myopic loss aversion. [192]

This is, therefore, one of the richer paragraphs in behavioural finance content throughout Vega's book, as it reflects various concepts. The next paragraph contains a very enigmatic challenge to prospect theory:

> "[…] even the wealthiest men are forced to buy stocks, and there are people who do not sell them when the prices have fallen, in order to avoid a loss. But they do not sell at rising prices either [to protect a gain], because they do not know a more secure investment for their capital." (De la Vega, 1957, 13, para 92)

---

excerpt from the original Spanish edition of *Confusion of Confusions* (cited by Corzo et al., 2014 and not included in the Kellenbenz-translation) on the various sources of regret in investors' decisions:

"Some people are always unhappy. If they have bought and the prices fall, they are unhappy because they bought; if the prices rise, they are unhappy because they did not buy more. If they have sold they are unhappy because they sold for less than they could have; if they did not buy or sell, they are unhappy because they did not do anything; if they receive a tip and they did not follow it, they are also unhappy. Everything produces unhappiness." (para 51)

Regret in the above can be stronger ("If they have bought and the prices fall, they are unhappy because they bought"–implies they regret having done the wrong thing) or weaker ("if the prices rise, they are unhappy because they did not buy more"–implies they regret not having done more of the right thing). A similarly weaker regret is reflected through the "If they have sold they are unhappy because they sold for less than they could have" (it implies they did the right thing–sold at a profit–but could have done more of that right thing by waiting for prices to rise even more before selling). The last two parts of the excerpt relate to regret of one's inaction.

[192] It would also be expected to amplify the disposition effect mentioned earlier (investors would be more likely to sell their winners and hold onto their losers, given the wild swings in prices), in line with contemporary research evidence on the role of volatility in strengthening the disposition effect (Kumar, 2009; Dai et al., 2023).

Whereas the first sentence pertains to risk-seeking for losses coupled with loss-aversion ("there are people who do not sell them when the prices have fallen, in order to avoid a loss"), the second sentence reflects no risk-aversion for gains. Investors hold onto their stocks, because–presumably–no other investment in the Dutch market at the time offered a higher safety (or perhaps, even return).[193] The wording of Vega's quote (it begins with "even the wealthiest men") renders it likely that it refers more to the wealthy capital-holders of the Amsterdam Stock Exchange, who were (as mentioned in Chapter 2) more interested in securing a dividend income from their shareholdings, without feeling the need to speculate on price-differentials.[194]

Taken together, the above shows that, although the concept of prospect theory was not known in the 17th century, investors during that time behaved largely in line with it, thus tacitly confirming how closely prospect theory mirrors investors' decision-making in real life.

3.1.11 Satisficing

As mentioned in Chapter 1, key to the concept of the Economic Man is that he is presumed to be able to optimise in his decisions. In real life, however, optimising is not always possible, or (even if it is) the computational costs involved in attaining it (e.g., cost of information collection, cost of information processing, thinking etc.) are so large that render it less attractive. As a result, humans do not collect/process all information, thus bearing limitations in terms of their knowledge and its processing; this introduces boundaries to their rationality, in turn leading them to seek solutions that are satisfactory enough, without necessarily being optimal (Simon, 1959). This satisficing process involves choosing from among the available options the one with the least negative aspects (e.g., smallest cost). We also showed in Chapter 1 that satisficing is based on a host of biases and heuristics that allow humans to tackle the complexity of their surrounding environment.

---

193 Returns on bonds hovered around 7-8% (Gelderblom and Jonker, 2004), while interest on loans ranged between 2.5-3% per annum (De la Vega, 13, para 92). By comparison, the volatility of Dutch East India Company share-prices, allowed investors to realise double-digit returns within a day.

194 It is also not unlikely that wealthy capitalists in 17th century Netherlands felt compelled to hold Dutch East India Company shares due to the prestige conferred by holding shares of their country's "national trade champion"–a prestige which might also have helped confirm their social status in the context of the Dutch society's investment culture of the time; for more on the link of shareholdings with social prestige, see Rutterford et al. (2017).

On this issue, Vega shares the following quote:

> "Philosopher: [...] philosophy teaches . . . that the stomach cannot digest an excess of food, . . . and [accordingly] it is very sensible to be satisfied with [limited] profits, even if one does not gain all [possible] riches and advantages." (De la Vega, 1957, 15, para 100)

Vega's quote above should be placed in the wider context of rampant speculation and volatility of the 17th century Amsterdam Stock Exchange described in his book. As per paragraph 66:

> "The second principle: Take every gain without showing remorse about missed profits, because an eel may escape sooner than you think. It is wise to enjoy that which is possible without hoping for the continuance of a favorable conjuncture and the persistence of good luck." (De la Vega, 1957, 10, para 66)

> "The third principle: Profits on the exchange are the treasures of goblins. At one time they may be carbuncle stones, then coals, then diamonds, then flint-stones, then morning dew, then tears." (De la Vega, 1957, 10, para 66)

In essence, Vega advocates satisficing, by advising that investors be content with *some* profit and not feel regret about not attaining the *optimal* profit. Vega's satisficing-nudge in paragraph 100 largely hinges on the extreme uncertainty involved in equity investing in his time; as investors may have often found equity trading daunting amid this uncertainty (more so, given the nascent concepts of the stock exchange and equity trading, both pioneered in 17th century Amsterdam), the best thing to do would have been to pocket any profit early on, rather than entertain long-term profit expectations.

3.1.12 Sentiment

The notion of sentiment in finance relates to extrapolative beliefs about future cash flows and risks; these beliefs, though based on the perception of a trend being at works (e.g., that an up/downward trend in earnings will persist), are not necessarily supported by facts (Baker and Wurgler, 2007). Although the beliefs underlying sentiment can be founded on fundamentals (which are extrapolated upon to project future trends), this does not mean that these fundamentals are processed rationally. Investors can envisage future growth rates, for example, by extrapolating on patterns from historical ones (see e.g., the model proposed by Barberis et al., 1998). As a result, sentiment can prompt investors to overreact to news, often giving rise to bubbles of various types in the process.[195] Sentiment-shifts can be motivated by both affective sources (e.g., emotions), as well as non-affective ones (e.g., shifts in our attention, or extrapolative expectations; Peng and Xiong, 2006; Barberis et al., 2018). Sentiment involves an amount of cognitive effort in its formulation–an effort that is, nevertheless, mediated by behavioural biases and heuristics, hence denoting sentiment's relation to noise trader activity. This relation has, however, been challenged by recent evidence (e.g.., DeVault et al., 2018) suggesting that many popular sentiment indicators may in fact be capturing institutional demand; furthermore, ample research (e.g., De Long et al., 1990a; Brunnermeier, 2008; Liao et al., 2011; Chau et al., 2016) indicates that rational investors can speculate on sentiment to exploit their noise peers.

Vega offers the first known reference to sentiment in equity trading history by referring to "Bulls" and "Bears" in the Amsterdam Stock Exchange. Compared to the behavioural finance definition of sentiment representing bullish/bearish tendencies at the market-wide level, Vega's Bulls and Bears bore a narrower connotation, corresponding to specific groups of traders aiming at profiting from taking long (the Bulls) or short (the Bears) positions in the market (see the discussion in the previous chapter). As Vega describes them:

> "It is particularly worth remarking that in this gambling hell there are two classes of speculators who are so opposed to one another that they represent antipodes in their decisions and, as I believe, in their destinies. The first class consists of the bulls or liejhebberen (the latter meaning "lovers" in Flemish). They are those members of the Exchange who start their operations by purchases, just as if they were lovers of the country, of the state, and of the Company. They always desire a rise in the price of the shares; they hope that by reason of good news the market will be suddenly stirred up, and that prices will rise high rapidly. The second faction consists of the bears or the

---

[195] An example of a sentiment-amplified bubble is an intrinsic bubble; this refers to a bubble that depends on fundamentals (i.e., fundamentals are endogenous to it). In this case, the more fundamentals improve, the more investors are convinced that pricing is in the right direction and, hence the more the bubble grows. Such bubbles are strongly motivated by the representativeness heuristic (see Chapter 1), whereby people attach higher probabilities to states of the world that are representative of the observed news (Gennaioli et al., 2015). In this case, people overestimate the probability of an outcome or a state of the world, if the data/news render it more likely (or appear more stereotypical of it). If a bubble is in process, we therefore tend to overweight good news (that supports the bubble's continuation) and downplay bad news–or, indeed, any losses or risk (since they are incongruent with the bubble's narrative).

contremine (a name which is explained by the fact that India is considered to be a mine and that this faction strives to exhaust this mine). The bears always begin operations with sales. […] [The bulls] love everything, they praise everything, they exaggerate everything. And as Bias deceived the ambassador of Alyattes during the siege of Priene by showing him hills of sand covered with wheat and intimating to him that such a wealthy town would never surrender because of famine, so the bulls make the public believe that their tricks signify wealth and that crops grow on graves. […] The bears, on the contrary, are completely ruled by fear, trepidation, and nervousness. Rabbits become elephants, brawls in a tavern become rebellions, faint shadows appear to them as signs of chaos. But if there are sheep in Africa that are supposed to serve as donkeys and wethers to serve even as horses, what is there miraculous about the likelihood that every dwarf will become a giant in the eyes of the bears?" (De la Vega, 1957, 12, para 82)

As the above illustrate, sentiment in 17th century equity trading in Amsterdam was shaped by interest-groups with opposing directions in their speculation, motivated strongly by disagreements as per Dutch East India Company's policies and management.[196] Therefore, although sentiment was undoubtedly fuelled by unsophisticated investors who jumped onto the bandwagon of the Bulls or the Bears, the source of this sentiment appears to rest within more informed (involving corporate insiders) circles in the market.

Bulls and Bears responded differently to the same information:

"In order that you should not come to the conclusion that the movements of the stock exchange are inexplicable and that nothing is firm, take note and realize that there are three causes of a rise in the prices on the exchange and three of a fall: the conditions in India, European politics, and opinion on the stock exchange itself. For this last reason the news [as such] is often of little value, since counteracting forces [may] operate in the opposite direction." (De la Vega, 1957, 9, para 65)

However, they also tended to focus on different information too, contingent on their own best interests:

"[…] one portion of the speculators would buy on the strength of the Indian news, while another sells on the basis of the unclear European situation." (De la Vega, 1957, 9, para 66)

---

[196] See the discussion in Chapter 2.

As a result, there existed two *ad hoc* sentiment-shaping forces in the market and Vega now recommends something that comes very close to sentiment-driven trading/speculation:

> "Eudicus tells that in Hestiaeotis there were two wells called Ceron and Melan and that, if the sheep drank from the first, they became white; if they drank from the second, they became black; and, if from both together, they got different colors as interesting as agreeable to the eye. If you wish to succeed in your enterprises, don't drink continually of the well of the liefhebberen because it is no good to be white; but don't drink always from the well of the contreminers either, for it is never good to be black as a raven. ... In short, not always Melan and not always Ceron, but always speculate for a rise from natural inclination and on a fall only on occasion, because experience has shown that usually the bulls are victorious and the bears lose out." (De la Vega, 1957, 12-13, para 89)

What Vega states here is that it is important for a successful trader to consider both sentiment-groups' opinions when formulating his strategy, without subscribing excessively to either of them. This comes very close to research evidence (e.g., Liao et al., 2011; Chau et al., 2016) on some investors adopting strategies that speculate on market sentiment.

The above, therefore, denote the birth of the bullish/bearish sentiment terminology in *Confusion of Confusions*; as Vega showcases, sentiment was largely driven by groups with vested, yet opposing, interests in the Dutch East India Company. These groups employed a host of manipulative schemes and machinations to further their interests, as so amply presented in the book's *Fourth Dialogue*. Given that the company's policies were not dictated by corporate insiders (e.g., its board) only, but also the Dutch government amid an era of global colonial competition (see Chapter 2), this suggests that sentiment in Vega's time was politically (in the broad sense of the term) motivated, with each group (Bulls; Bears) trying to sway the masses of small investors into trading directions suiting its interests.

3.1.13 Trade-based manipulation

Trade-based manipulation refers to the trading practice involving buying and selling shares without releasing rumours or engaging into any actions to impact the actual value of the company (Allen and Gale, 1992).[197] Vega

---

[197] Allen and Gale (1992) contrast this to other types of manipulation involving changing the value of a company (action-based manipulation) or releasing rumors ("pump and dump" or information-based manipulation). See also the manipulation-taxonomy proposed by Putniņš (2012).

offers a series of examples (mostly in the *Fourth Dialogue*) relevant to trade-based manipulation, which we shall discuss in turn:

> "[…] it is possible for owners of East shares to be freed from their engagements in order to strengthen their position in "West", and vice versa. If the stock exchange turns away from one variety of share in order to favor the other, and if many shares of one kind are sold against cash in order to push up the price of the other, either by purchasing the other stock outright or by loaning to other speculators through hypothecation of their purchases, the speculators fear a sudden fall [in the price of the first stock], and they become depressed from fear of further attacks. Therefore they speed up their sales [of this second stock]; the zest for this paper diminishes, and its price falls." (De la Vega, 1957, 20, para 195)

What is described here is speculators switching positions between Dutch East India Company and Dutch West India Company shares, with proceeds from the sales of one used to finance positions in the other. The above describes a case whereby speculators try to make a profit by combining positions in two assets, a practice established in the modern literature (see e.g., Kumar and Seppi, 1992) and recently (Griffin and Shams, 2020) documented in cryptocurrencies.[198]

> "Although the bears lack shares, they do not blush to create the appearance of an abundance. The shares change hands, often fifty times in one week, rising and falling like balls [in a game], but this changing of hands is indicative only of the ruin of the business in shares. . . . What meaning does it have that the bears buy one share, when, protected by their alliance, they sell ten shares? What does it mean when they take over the hypothecated shares in order to pass them out again immediately? […] Would scholars consider incorrect [a statement to the effect] that I cannot regard the purchase of one share a [bona fide] purchase when four are sold simultaneously, that I cannot consider a [bona fide] taking-up of one share [any transaction which entails that] ten shares be delivered simultaneously?" (De la Vega, 1957, 32, para 293)

Again here, this is reflective of trade-based manipulation by combining purchases and sales of shares; specifically, what is described here comes very close to the modern definition of spoofing, which involves traders taking actions to project a false impression of trading interest in a security. Spoofing involves several aspects; those relevant to Vega's narrative here

---

[198] This practice may also involve some sort of pair-trading, whereby investors enter and exit positions between two stocks when a ratio reflective of a relationship between some feature of theirs (e.g., volume or price) crosses a certain threshold.

are a) entering fictitious orders (involves entering orders on the buy (sell) side, completing a sell (buy) order and then deleting the original buy (sell) order after the trade has been completed) and b) switches (you place a buy (sell) order, then delete it as it approaches priority and then enter a sell (buy) order).[199]

> "Eleventhly, the Contremine [i.e., the syndicate] carries out the following trick in order to reach its aim: they are not content to wound their enemies with their tongue, which Jeremiah compares to an arrow, and to fight them with their teeth . . .and with arguments. In order to insinuate that their own concern is founded on grave considerations and does not refer exclusively to the situation of the Company, the bears sell government obligations. Thus the bulls are to be made to believe that discord is dominating the state and that there is a reason to be alarmed about and to pay attention to a possible outbreak of war. […] This recourse to selling long and short-term state obligations may seem to be of but small importance for the business [in stocks], but whoever thinks so is in error. . . . Our speculators [i.e., the bulls] are paralyzed in their stock dealings, and are bled by their engagements [to protect the market] in state bonds, [all because of a trumped-up allegation of a] situation perilous to the country, dangers threatening the Company, and a break down of the share market." (De la Vega, 1957, 33, para 305)

The above description involves trading in two asset classes, to use trading in one to generate gains in the other. Bears started selling government bonds to create an impression of an impending crisis, thus prompting the Bulls to divert funds from the stock market to the bond market (thus rendering it easier for the Bears to corner the stock market).

> "One of the neatest tricks which take place in these circles is for some of the bulls to pose as bears. This is done for two reasons. First, because the opponents [the real bears] imagine that, if they [are able to] buy a share from among those held back and concealed, the other party [that of the bulls] has changed its ideas and, instead of building silver bridges for them, seek to drag them down. . . Now the bulls change the price so that they [the bears] are forced to pay dearly for the shares which they have sold short [in their attempt to subdue the bulls]. Thus the bulls reach their aim, and thus they defeat their malevolent enemies through pretence, and thus by cautious manoeuvres they deceive these opponents who are trying to deceive them." (De la Vega, 1957, 35, para 323)

In the above, Bulls perform a few initial sales (something unexpected, given Bull's aversion to selling) to prompt Bears to believe that Bulls have

199 For more on spoofing, see Putniņš (2020).

a serious reason to sell and start selling short; once this happens, Bulls bid up the price, leading Bears to suffer losses.[200]

The following excerpt reflects a modified version of ramping/gouging– a manipulative tactic, whereby the manipulator (normally a broker, or a set of colluding brokers) enters purchase orders for a stock at successively higher prices, in order to generate the impression that the stock enjoys particularly high interest:

> "[…] some such speculators, operating under the pretext of trying to please a broker, are friendly with him (without really intending to be of real advantage to the latter). They give him an order to buy one or several shares, but at the moment of execution they appear on the Exchange themselves and offer a higher rate than they had authorized the unfortunate broker to bid, whom they had thus deceived by cajolery. What is the use of giving an order, if in the same moment means are sought to prevent its execution?" (De la Vega, 1957, 23, para 224)

We now turn to the following from paragraph 305:

> "In order to be well-informed about the tendency of the market, even the bears [before launching their big operation] begin with purchases and take all items [offered]. If the shares rise in price, they pocket the quick profit; if the prices fall, however, they sell at a loss, content to have ascertained the weakening tendency. Moreover, the interest which the timid public takes in their proceedings is already useful to them, since the public thinks that conditions must be serious when the speculators sell at a loss. This is one of the most powerful available stratagems for influencing the wavering elements. If [the timid souls] see the bears buy, they do not know whether the latter buy in order to sell later (which in the Exchange language means to "look for powder"), or whether they buy because they have changed their opinion or given up their position and therefore really want to buy. If the Contremine decides upon this dissimulation, they offer for the stocks more than the price of the day (what we call "inflating" the price). They influence the price in this way in order to sell [short] at the higher figure and thus to gain in the end." (De la Vega, 1957, 33, para 305)

We left this excerpt for the end of this sub-section's discussion, since it constitutes a special case, as it reflects trade-based manipulation motivated by rational speculation. The latter was analytically calibrated by De Long et al. (1990a), who proposed a model involving two trader-types: rational

[200] Short-selling involves selling an asset you do not currently own, with the obligation of buying it back at some point in the future, the expectation therefore being that its price will fall (to buy it back cheap). If Bulls bid up the price, Bears would have to buy the shorted shares back at higher prices, hence at a loss for them.

speculators and noise traders (who extrapolate from historical price-trends). In their model-setting, rational speculators witness a signal indicating that good news about a stock will arrive to the market in the near future; armed with this knowledge, they choose to pre-empt the market (and rationally thinking), they buy the stock, whose price (predictably enough) starts rising. Noise traders witness the uptrend in the stock's price and start buying too (since they base their trades on past prices), leading the stock's price to retain its upward momentum. When the good news arrives at the market, rational speculators decide to sell the stock and, at the same time, go short on it. Selling the stock when the good news hits the market makes sense; with noise traders having boosted the upward trend, the price probably has risen by now far beyond what the good piece of news implied (see what we mentioned earlier about overreaction).

Why do rational speculators go short at the same time, though? As soon as they start selling, they know the price will start declining and they know that noise traders will pick up on the observed down-trend (since past price-trends inform their trades) and follow it by unloading their positions. This will put price-pressure over the stock, depressing its price even more (and render their short-selling more profitable). In this way, rational speculators pocket profits from two different legs of their strategy:

a) The long leg (by selling their long position in the stock upon the news' arrival) and

b) The short leg by simultaneously selling the stock short

In this way, rational speculators exploit their informational superiority– and their noise counterparts, in the process, by front-running their anticipated trades.

Paragraph 305 is directly relevant to the concept of rational speculation; as soon as the Bears practice their misdirection by buying shares (something unexpected, since investors associate Bears with sales), some investors will enter the price-momentum by buying more. At some point, the bears unload their short positions and a price-collapse ensues. As a result, Vega describes (almost verbatim in spirit) the model-context of De Long et al. (1990a)– which forms a special case of trade-based manipulation.[201]

The above, therefore, suggest that trade-based manipulation was commonplace in Amsterdam's stock market during the 17th century. Practiced widely (courtesy of the speculative fervour in the Dutch market at

[201] There is one subtle difference between what is described in Vega and what De Long et al. (1990a) explore. Whereas Vega's rational speculators in paragraph 305 need not necessarily exploit their informational superiority (it is not clear from the paragraph whether their trades are motivated by information or not), De Long et al. (1990a)'s prey on noise investors by taking advantage of their own private signals.

the time), it assumed a variety of forms very similar to those encountered in contemporary settings and analysed in the finance literature.

3.2 Concluding remarks

Confusion of Confusions is, in effect, not just the first primer on stock trading and investors' behaviour–it is also the precursor to behavioural finance. Putting together his book in discursive form, Vega assumes the role of the Shareholder to educate his two companions, the Merchant and the Philosopher, on issues of investments; Vega's ambition when writing this book was threefold, as Kellenbenz notes:

> "The author stressed in the preface to his book that he had three motives in writing the dialogues: first, his own pleasure; again, for those who were not active in the trade, he desired to describe a business which was on the whole the most honest and most useful of all that existed at that time; and, lastly, he wished to describe accurately and fully the tricks that rascals knew how to employ in that business." (De la Vega, 1957, xi)

What Vega, however achieved (without ever suspecting it) was to put together the first known treatise on behavioural finance issues–issues that were only systemised/formalised around 300 years after he had finished writing his book. Key to the value of *Confusion of Confusions* is that it was written in an era devoid of modern-day technological luxuries that allow traders to perform their transactions through their screens, without even physically interacting with their peers. Vega was, in some capacity, a fortunate man: he experienced investment life in the world's first organised stock exchange and this allowed him to record how investors behaved when equity trading was only a nascent innovation. Experiencing investment life at the Amsterdam Stock Exchange first-hand from the inside allowed him to witness investors' judgements, their decisions, and their errors, as they experimented with trading stocks. Going beyond mere description, his narrative offers critical insights into the workings of investors' minds and motives, discussing aspects of their behaviour that would only be academically investigated three centuries later.

Let us now try to provide a summative behavioural finance assessment of the Amsterdam stock market based on Vega's narrative. A large part of the Dutch market's trader-population of the time comprised of noise, uninformed investors, eager to speculate (some more than others) through a novel business (equity trading). A fraction of them were more informed–at least to varying degrees; these were corporate insiders, members of the business community, wealthy capitalists, and brokers. What "informed" meant back then is hard to ascertain, considering the ambivalent fundamentals, the opaque accounting practices of the Dutch East India Company and the lack of communication technologies (which implied that news arrived with a certain delay–courtesy of which it could easily become obsolete). Presumably corporate insiders (e.g., company directors) had more access to information, though inside information did not exclusively predominate the market; what Vega describes is a market laden with noisy signals–and rumours. As a result, fundamentals-driven trading, in the modern sense of the term, had little scope in such a market. The prevalent informational ambiguity and the nascent innovation represented by equity trading gave rise to short-term speculation[202] and wider social participation by members of the public. As this implied a proliferation of noise trading, it was perhaps inevitable for the market to grow in volume and volatility–and for behavioural patterns to arise. Hence, traders chased trends, herded behind the trades of their peers, overreacted to news and were very much susceptible to manipulative schemes (whose instigators often resorted to various attention-grabbing tactics to attract investors). They were eager to gamble (especially in the face of losses) and were faced with sentiment-shifts, which potentially contradicted their own analyses/opinions when choosing to trade. Their strategies were largely based on non-fundamentals, and, when fundamentals-related news did arrive, they often exhibited disagreement in its interpretation. Consequently, investors in 17th century Amsterdam projected behavioural patterns in their trades that Vega eloquently documents for the first time in the history of stock trading–patterns that were touched upon academically in the 20th century.

If a modern-day trader were to, hypothetically, go back in time to 17th century Amsterdam and enter its stock exchange, he would likely come across behavioural elements in investors' trades far from alien to him. If a behavioural researcher were to undertake the same time-travel, he probably would rejoice, as he would find himself in a trading environment accommodating consistent and recurring departures from rationality worth studying. In the end, *Confusion of Confusions* showcases that humans' basic instincts have not changed; investors today judge, decide, behave, err, and think in ways very similar to those of their 17th century peers. Much of the difference in investors' behaviour across the span of these three centuries is simply one of degree and evolution (primarily institutional and technological).

---

[202] See, for example, what Vega mentions about ducaton-trading: "One rarely agrees in this business to a transaction with a longer time to run than one month, because the resources of the people concerned are not sufficient" (De la Vega, 1957, 27, para 239).

At this point, one might argue that the above strike a pessimistic tone; after all, if after over 300 years we still make the same mistakes, this suggests we are not (good enough in) learning. If this is what the reader concludes from our discussion, he will be delighted to know that behavioural finance research confirms his suspicions. Our learning is impeded by biases that distort inputs and lessons from our experiences; the impact of these biases prevails in the face of education, repetition, experience and strong incentives–even among investors otherwise deemed sophisticated (e.g., Menkhoff and Nikiforov, 2009). In the end, some biases are just too potent to eliminate; a typical example is overconfidence, which can bias the updating of one's self-assessment, even when newly incoming information about one's ability is not favourable (Hirshleifer, 2015). This updating is further hampered by reinforcement learning; people place much more weight on their own past experiences, preferring to downplay information. With reinforcement learning, previous choices are more (less) likely to be repeated, if they were proven successful (unsuccessful), something that has been too often confirmed in financial decisions.[203] In addition, people do not learn because they may not be bothered to; inertia and habits may prove stronger, particularly when stability reigns in their environment, in which case, relying on habits (such as reinforcement learning) or defaults can lead to constrained optimal outcomes (Samuelson and Zeckhauser 1988; Hirshleifer and Welch 2002; Payzan-LeNestour, 2023).[204]

Perhaps, then, this is the most important contribution of Vega's work; it reminds us that we cannot escape from the fundamentals of our very human nature and that, no matter how much we (think we) have evolved, we never really stray far from it.[205] In the next chapter we shall explore some implications of this.

---

[203] The case of re-buying stocks that were previously sold for a gain (Barber et al., 2014) or participating in an IPO, if your track record of previous IPO-investments has been positive (Kaustia and Knüpfer, 2008).

[204] This is not likely, however, to be the case when stability ceases to exist; when that happens, the stability-momentum breaks and the individual now has to expend effort to learn about the fundamentals of the new regime of affairs.

[205] This notion, namely that humans are prone to persistent errors due to their nature has been at the focus of much recent research in the inter-disciplinary domain of neurofinance; drawing on neuroscientific technologies (in mostly controlled settings), neurofinance researchers have demonstrated that our choices under risk and uncertainty (and the valuation of those choices) are significantly influenced by our emotions (as they often tend to trigger the activation of brain-regions associated with affect). For a recent discussion on this, see Payzan-LeNestour (2023).

CHAPTER 4

CONFUSION OF CONFUSIONS: IMPLICATIONS

Confusion of Confusions provides a first-hand account of investment life in the 1680s' Amsterdam Stock Exchange, with its narrative revealing a series of aspects of investors' behaviour at the time–aspects that were later crystallised into concrete concepts only during the last quarter of the 20th century, amid the evolution of behavioural finance since the 1980s. In the previous chapter, we critically assessed Vega's book from the perspective of the behavioural finance paradigm and showed that (absent the possibility of the discovery in the future of a text of similar content written pre-1688) it certainly qualifies as the precursor to modern-day behavioural finance. We now turn to explore the book's implications for various stakeholders. At this point, one might argue that *Confusion of Confusions* is vastly obsolete and naturally outdated, having little more to offer than the astute observations of a market participant from a time long forgotten. Although such an argument would imply that we have little to learn from Vega, this chapter will demonstrate that reality is a bit more complex than that.

4.1 Implications for research

A key implication of *Confusion of Confusions* is that it helps backdate a series of behavioural biases/heuristics/trading patterns, as our discussion in Chapter 3 has revealed. Although prior literature on pre 20th century markets has largely alluded to the presence of mass psychology phenomena (such as bubbles and herding), it did so without focusing on more specific traits of investors' psychology.[206] Vega's book allows us insights into several biases and heuristics from the formative years of the world's very first organised stock exchange. To that end, his book offers the first documented description of such psychological traits in investment practice that we know of.

---

[206] For narrative evidence on investors' herding in historical stock exchanges, see the discussion in Gavriilidis and Kallinterakis (2023) and references therein.

A second key implication of his book is that it helps open up new research directions (and the revisiting of existing ones) for behavioural finance research. This stems from the fact that the manifestation of several biases and heuristics in his narrative entails features that have received limited/no attention in research to date. To elaborate on this, we will outline a few examples based on our discussion in Chapter 3:

- The speculation described for Dutch East India Company shares took place in the presence of pronounced dividend uncertainty, in terms of both the regularity of dividend payments, as well as their type (since they were often paid in kind). A question arising is whether/how variations in dividend uncertainty motivate variations in investors' behaviour. For example, how would the significance of behavioural trading patterns be expected to vary between stocks with high-versus-low levels of dividend uncertainty?[207]
- Vega often alludes to the presence of herding in manipulative schemes (see section 3.1.5), yet there is little research currently on this. Although herding is intuitively innate to such schemes (manipulation thrives when many investors are attracted in the direction of the manipulated asset), how herding varies across the various stages of manipulation is a notably under-researched topic.
- In section 3.1.6, Vega implies the presence of a high-volume return premium for Amsterdam-traded stocks (versus stocks traded in the other five chambers, which enjoyed lower volume and speculation). Although volume and speculation are noise-related (see e.g., Black, 1986), research has yet to explore the relation between behavioural trading patterns (and their variations) with the high-volume return premium.
- The fact that noise trading was amplified for ducatons (see section 3.1.7) raises the possibility of something similar occurring for other fractional assets in modern markets. Examples here would be fractional positions in cryptocurrencies and stocks; given the higher likelihood of fractional positions hailing from investors of lower sophistication, one might expect stronger behavioural trading patterns to arise from their part–an issue that, as of yet, has received limited attention (Da et al., 2021; Bartlett et al., 2022; Tripathi and Rengifo, 2023).

---

[207] For example, since dividends constitute inputs for the calculation of a firm's fundamental value, a testable hypothesis here would be that higher dividend uncertainty (in terms of regularity and/or type) motivates greater recourse to behavioural trading among investors.

- Continuing from the previous point, one might wonder whether a scheme similar to what speculators had devised for the trading between ducatons and large shares of the Dutch East India Company might be feasible today for fractional positions in stocks or cryptocurrencies. Assuming e.g., the example of Bitcoin, one could enter fractional Bitcoin positions in exchanges where Bitcoin is priced at lower values, wait until those positions appreciate in value versus the actual value of their fraction of Bitcoin, and then unload them to buy whole Bitcoin units in exchanges where Bitcoin is less expensive. Although arbitrage has been studied for cryptocurrencies across different exchanges,[208] the role of fractional positions in this context has not been studied to date–and it would be interesting to see whether a 17th century pattern holds nowadays.

The above examples denote that *Confusion of Confusions* does raise issues of investors' behaviour that have not been (widely) touched upon by behavioural finance researchers.[209]

A third implication (stemming from the previous two) pertains to the importance of financial history in the study and understanding of investors' behaviour. Since Vega helps us backdate biases/heuristics and entails behavioural finance issues under- or unexplored, this suggests that behavioural researchers could consider exploring various facets of investors' behaviour in stock exchanges from previous centuries. Admittedly, an issue certain to arise here is one of feasibility: data of even the simplest form (e.g., prices) are extremely hard to come by (assuming they even exist). This leads historical finance research to focus on a very narrow subset of markets for which such data exists (data which may well be incomplete, or involve limited subsets of stocks).[210] Despite this, it is worth noting that a series of

---

208 For more on cryptocurrency arbitrage, see the discussion and references in Crépellière et al. (2023).

209 Beyond research ideas, *Confusion of Confusions* could further be utilised as recommended reading for under/postgraduate and doctoral economics/finance students (particularly those with a focus on behavioural economics/finance in their studies/research) as a simple introduction to several aspects of investors' behaviour.

210 A good source of historical data for a very limited sample of markets, including the US, the UK, pre-Communist Russia and pre-Communist China can be found on the website of the International Finance Center of the Yale School of Management (https://som.yale.edu/centers/international-center-for-finance/data/historical-financial-research-data). Beyond that (and a few other proprietary databases), researchers in historical finance rely largely on hand-collected data from digitised copies of financial newspapers of the time, a largely time-consuming, manual-entry task. For examples of discussions of such databases, see Vaihekoski (2022) and Lehmann-Hasemeyer and Opitz (2024).

modern-day stylised return-patterns have been studied in pre-20th century markets, including, for example, mean reversion (e.g., Annaert and Van Hyfte, 2004), liquidity premium (e.g., Gernandt et al., 2012), equity premium (e.g., Annaert et al., 2015) and asymmetric volatility (e.g., Goetzmann et al., 2001).[211] With regards to behavioural finance patterns, the output is relatively limited, primarily involving herding (Bohl et al., 2012; Kallinterakis and Gavriilidis, 2023), feedback trading (Pierdzioch, 2004), momentum (Annaert and Mensah, 2014; Geczy and Samonov, 2016; Goetzmann and Huang, 2018), and home bias (Acheson and Turner, 2011; Rutterford et al., 2017). This suggests that academic research on behavioural finance issues from pre-20th century markets is relatively nascent and merits greater interest, data permitting. One possibility for behavioural finance researchers to tackle the data-issue is to forge collaborations with colleagues of theirs from historical finance research (since these will be likely to have access to some historical data).

A fourth implication involves the role of historical finance texts (similar to *Confusion of Confusions*) in contributing to our understanding of investors' behaviour. Similar to Vega's book, behavioural finance scholars could indulge in unearthing and reading similar texts from past centuries and draw on them for insights that may enrich our understanding of contemporary behavioural trading patterns–and motivate new research ideas.

4.2 Implications for investors

An investor benefits from reading Vega's book in several ways. First, she gets to see that investors in the 17th century were committing errors of judgement remarkably similar to those witnessed among modern-day investors. This may lead her to realise that the fundamentals of human nature have hardly changed over the course of three centuries, and leave the impression that she can fall prey to such errors too; if so, this can help her guard against overconfidence (among other biases) in her trading and encourage introspection in investment decision-making.[212] This is further

[211] For more details and additional references, see Gavriilidis and Kallinterakis (2023).

[212] This is, of course, only one possibility; alternatively, an investor reading Vega's book may reach the erroneous conclusion that 17th century investors' errors of judgement do not apply to 21st century investors, due to the latter being of superior sophistication (e.g., due to the technological tools available to them). Unfortunately for that investor, modern financial history contains one example too many of

facilitated by the fact that *Confusion of Confusions* is largely non-technical, relying on a discursive style (almost like a theatrical play) devoid of any normative message (it contains no explicit directives for investment decisions), thus helping the reader grow more receptive to Vega's advice.

A second implication of the book for the investor is that it offers an indirect introduction to behavioural finance; this can potentially invigorate her interest in learning more about the discipline and educating herself about investors' behaviour, something clearly beneficial in self-development terms. If the investor exposes herself more broadly to behavioural finance research, this can allow her to utilise inputs from the latter in her investment strategies and prompt her to reflect more on her trades, thus leading to better calibrated decisions.[213]

4.3 Implications for investment practitioners

Confusion of Confusions can be utilised by financial advisors with the purpose of furthering their clients' (financial) education by asking them to read it and then discuss certain topical points of direct concern or relevance to them. The non-technical nature of the book ensures its accessibility to investors of various backgrounds of financial knowledge and the book is likely to constitute a helpful discussion-trigger between advisors and their clients. This is expected to be more so, given its ease of pitching to the latter as the first book ever written on stock market investments (which would be expected to arouse their curiosity and motivate their attention).

Financial psychologists could also consider utilising Vega's book for their practice. To the extent that it refers to investors' errors of judgement from the distant past, it might help their clients feel less negative about themselves/their own investment experiences (since it would make them realise how intact the fundamentals of human nature have remained over time) and hence grow more receptive to the idea of engaging openly about them.

---

recurrent episodes of investor irrationality (see e.g., Andrikopoulos et al., 2021), thus confirming that "there is no new thing under the sun".

[213] How beneficial this will be, will largely depend, of course, on how successful and bias-free her learning is–considering that learning is not homogeneous among individuals. After all, making (the same) mistakes and not (always) learning from them is what has fostered the advancement of behavioural finance as well the self-help finance literature, thus suggesting that we do try to understand and–possibly–learn, regardless of how successful we are in doing so.

4.4 Implications for regulators and policymakers

A major implication of Vega's work is its educational value and how it can be harnessed by regulators and policymakers in investors' education. *Confusion of Confusions* certainly qualifies as an entertaining narrative of investment life in the Amsterdam of Vega's time; to that end (and in line with what we mentioned in the previous sub-sections), it could be included in the curricula of financial literacy programmes. Given its non-technical nature, it is far more appealing/accessible to a wider audience, compared to more technical texts; its discursive/descriptive style can deliver clear messages to the reader, as it tacitly (and, oftentimes, explicitly) navigates through various behavioural themes by narration (e.g., vivid story-telling with recourse to historical parables), as well as example (by entering into details of the workings of the stock exchange and its participants). Vega's book could enter financial education curricula, either on its own (e.g., via the design of courses based on it) or as support material (e.g., for courses on behavioural finance, investments, derivatives etc.).

However, the most important implication of Vega's book for regulators and policymakers, rests in its educational value for *them*. If there is one thing that Vega demonstrates, it is that human nature does not change and that it has to be accepted for what it is. This casts doubts over normative regulatory approaches (which view regulation as the panacea to any market imperfection caused by investors' behaviour), implying the necessity for regulatory approaches of a more positive nature (i.e., which account for investors' behaviour into their design).[214] It also lends credence and support to the importance of nudging in policymaking (e.g., Thaler and Sunstein, 2009); exploiting investors' cognitive biases in designing choices for them can elicit more desirable behaviour on their part, compared e.g., to issuing them with explicit directives (in the hope of people following them)[215], or

---

[214] Normative approaches to regulation presume that imperfections or irrationalities can be corrected via regulation. The key issue with such approaches is that, beyond ignoring the roots of investors' deviations from rationality, they also ignore the fact that regulators themselves are also prone to biases in their judgement, behaviour and motives. With regards to the latter, evidence (e.g., Gerding, 2006) denotes that regulation tends to follow a cyclical trajectory, growing more (less) stringent during bearish (bullish) markets, where sentiment turns pessimistic (optimistic) and investors are more likely to be faced with losses (gains) and, hence more (less) likely to demand regulatory intervention. For more on positive regulatory approaches, see Hirshleifer (2008).

[215] Issuing directives may motivate resistance against them.

expecting them to make the right choice on their own free will.[216] In view of the above, it might further be worth considering introducing the book to continuing professional education programmes in regulatory and policymaking agencies, in order for members of such bodies to be reminded of the importance of accounting for human nature when formulating policies.

4.5 Implications for the Sephardi community

The fact that *Confusion of Confusions* has been shown to constitute the precursor to modern-day behavioural finance bears also important implications for the Sephardi Jewish community in terms of cultural heritage/awareness. This is a community that has produced a series of writers on issues of economics and finance during the Renaissance years and beyond, some of whom are more famous than others. Examples of such names include Pedro de Santarém in insurance (Nogueira, 2002), Sarfatti de Pina in exchange rates (Nogueira, 2002; 2017), Isaac de Pinto (Nogueira, 2002) and David Ricardo (Heertje, 2015) in political economy, to mention but a few.

Vega is not entirely unknown as a scholarly figure; after all, some of his work (e.g., *"Asirei ha Tikva"*; see Chapter 2) has been praised for its impact over Jewish literary tradition of his time and beyond (see the discussion in Davidi, 2019a; b). Our critical analysis of *Confusion of Confusions* accentuates an additional (and under-recognised) impact of his work: being the first writer ever to publish a book on various aspects of investors' behaviour presented in a way impressively similar to that of modern behavioural finance research, Vega deserves to be formally acknowledged as the earliest known forerunner of behavioural finance. This forms an additional scholarly distinction for Vega that earns him a position among the abovementioned Sephardi contributors of his era to the broader field of economics and finance.

[216] The imperfections in human knowledge and judgement suggest that individuals may truly not be aware of what the right choice in any context is; even if they do, they may choose to ignore it, if e.g., it runs against their selfish interest or their personal beliefs.

EPILOGUE

When I first delved into *Confusion of Confusions* a few years ago, it felt very attractive to read, probably because of my background in behavioural finance research going back over two decades. The book contains lots of elements relevant to behavioural finance–and these we have been through in good detail. There is only one issue with Vega's book: nothing of what he discusses in there is really new. At least not for 21st century behavioural finance research; granted, with Amsterdam being the first organised stock exchange, what Vega describes in his book must have felt novel for his time. Or maybe not–we will never really know, given the lack of earlier texts describing the behaviour of investors in capital markets predating Amsterdam's[217]; as a result, *Confusion of Confusions* (for the moment, and until an older text of similar content is discovered) constitutes the first primer on investors' behaviour–and 1688 as the year when behavioural finance witnessed its dawn.

Coming back to what I mentioned before, nothing much of what is described in *Confusion of Confusions* is really new; investors behaved like textbook noise traders, chased rumours and trends (as well as other investors), jumped onto manipulation-schemes, participated in bubbles and crashes, and were eager to take on risks. The elements of behavioural finance included in Vega's book more or less match the coverage of modern-day modules on the subject. And all this, in an era whereby communication technology was virtually absent and people knew nothing about fundamentals (which also hovered between uncertainty and non-existence, pretty much like modern-day cryptocurrencies). If anything, it feels rather annoying knowing that investors in the 21st century commit the same errors of judgement initially reported in the behaviour of their peers over 330 years ago. Apparently, all the institutional and technological evolution witnessed since the years of the Enlightenment impacted us humans only on the surface (i.e., on which things we do and how we do them), yet not any deeper (i.e., why we do things–which involves our basic instincts comprising the foundations of our nature).

As a result, we are none the wiser when viewing our investment errors as special or unique; they are not. We never really stray far from our nature

[217] For examples of earlier forms of financial markets, see footnote 124.

in any realm of our lives–including that of investment decision-making, as Vega clearly shows. We project similar deviations from rationality in our behaviour over time and this means we are not (too) successful in learning. Maybe we are not even bothered to; after all, learning involves effort and this may be sufficient enough to deter us from learning (especially if the effort exceeds the expected benefit from learning).

Perhaps then this is the biggest takeaway from Vega's book: we need to accept human nature for what it is and moderate our expectations accordingly. The consistency of human nature ensures the recurrence of similar behaviours (in different packaging) over time and the cycle of events repeats itself. In the end:

> "The thing that hath been, it is that which shall be; and that which is done is that which shall be done: and there is no new thing under the sun. Is there any thing whereof it may be said, See, this is new? it hath been already of old time, which was before us. There is no remembrance of former things; neither shall there be any remembrance of things that are to come with those that shall come after." (Ecclesiastes 1:9-11)

BIBLIOGRAPHY

Abreu, Dilip, and Markus K. Brunnermeier. "Synchronization Risk and Delayed Arbitrage." Journal of Financial Economics 66, No. 2-3 (2002): 341–360.
https://doi.org/10.1016/S0304-405X(02)00227-1.

Abreu, Dilip, and Markus K. Brunnermeier. "Bubbles and Crashes." Econometrica 71, No. 1 (2003): pp.173–204.
https://doi.org/10.1111/1468-0262.00393.

Acheson, Graeme G., and John D. Turner. "Investor Behaviour in a Nascent Capital Market: Scottish Bank Shareholders in the Nineteenth Century." The Economic History Review 64, No. 1 (2011): 188–213.
http://www.jstor.org/stable/27919487.

Agarwal, Vikas, Lei Jiang, and Quan Wen. "Why Do Mutual Funds Hold Lottery Stocks?" Journal of Financial and Quantitative Analysis 57, No. 3 (2022): 825–56.
https://doi.org/10.1017/S0022109021000211.

Ajjoub, Carl, Thomas Walker, and Yunfei Zhao. "Social Media Posts and Stock Returns: The Trump Factor." International Journal of Managerial Finance 17, No. 2 (2021): 185-213.
https://doi.org/10.1108/IJMF-02-2020-0068.

Allen, Franklin, and Douglas Gale. "Stock-Price Manipulation." The Review of Financial Studies 5, No. 3 (1992): 503–29.
https://doi.org/10.1093/rfs/5.3.503.

Altanlar, Ali, Jiaqi Guo, and Phil Holmes. "Do Culture, Sentiment and Cognitive Dissonance Explain the "Above Suspicion" Anomalies?" European Financial Management 25, No. 5 (2019): 1168-1195.
http://dx.doi.org/10.1111/eufm.12203.

Alwathnani, Abdulaziz M., David A. Dubofsky, and Haitham A. Al-Zoubi. "Under-or-overreaction: Market Responses to Announcements of Earnings Surprises." International Review of Financial Analysis 52 (2017): 160-171.
https://doi.org/10.1016/j.irfa.2017.07.006.

Andrei, Daniel, and Michael Hasler. "Investor Attention and Stock Market Volatility." The Review of Financial Studies 28, No. 1 (2015): 33–72.
https://doi.org/10.1093/rfs/hhu059.

Andrikopoulos, Panagiotis, Bartosz Gebka, and Vasileios Kallinterakis. "Regulatory Mood-congruence and Herding: Evidence from Cannabis Stocks." Journal of Economic Behavior and Organization 185 (2021): 842-864.
https://doi.org/10.1016/j.jebo.2020.10.019.

Angel, James J., Raymond M. Brooks, and Prem G. Mathew. "When-Issued Shares, Small Trades, and the Variance of Returns Around Stock Splits." Journal of Financial Research 27, No. 3 (2004): 415-433.
https://doi.org/10.1111/j.1475-6803.2004.00094.x.

Annaert, Jan, Frans Buelens, and Marc Deloof. "Long-run Stock Returns: Evidence from Belgium 1838–2010." Cliometrica 9 (2015): 77–95.
https://doi.org/10.1007/s11698-014-0109-7.

Annaert, Jan and Lord Mensah. "Cross-sectional Predictability of Stock Returns, Evidence from the 19th Century Brussels Stock Exchange (1873–1914)." Explorations in Economic History 52 (2014): 22-43.
https://doi.org/10.1016/j.eeh.2013.10.002.

Annaert, Jan, and Wim Van Hyfte. "Long-horizon Mean Reversion for the Brussels Stock Exchange: Evidence for the 19th Century." SSRN Electronic Journal (December 20, 2004).
https://dx.doi.org/10.2139/ssrn.676006.

Ante, Lennart. "How Elon Musk's Twitter Activity Moves Cryptocurrency Markets." SSRN Electronic Journal (March 24th, 2022).
http://dx.doi.org/10.2139/ssrn.4065313.

Antoniou, Constantinos, John A. Doukas, and Avanidhar Subrahmanyam. "Cognitive Dissonance, Sentiment, and Momentum." Journal of Financial and Quantitative Analysis 48, No. 1 (2013): 245–75.
https://doi.org/10.1017/S0022109012000592.

Ardalan, Kavous. "Neurofinance versus the Efficient Markets Hypothesis." Global Finance Journal 35 (2018): 170-176.
https://doi.org/10.1016/j.gfj.2017.10.005.

Arnold, Marc, Matthias Pelstery, and Marti G. Subrahmanyam. "Attention Triggers and Investors' Risk Taking." Journal of Financial Economics 143, No. 2 (2022): 846-875.
https://doi.org/10.1016/j.jfineco.2021.05.031.

Assis, Yom Tov. 1988. The Jews of Spain: From Settlement to Expulsion. Jerusalem: The Hebrew University of Jerusalem.

Authers, John. "Number of Stock Indices at 3m Dwarfs Tally of Quoted Companies." The Financial Times, January 22, 2018.
https://www.ft.com/content/9ad80998-fed5-11e7-9650-9c0ad2d7c5b5.

Baker, Malcolm, Brendan Bradley, and Jeffrey Wurgler. "Benchmarks as Limits to Arbitrage: Understanding the Low-Volatility Anomaly." Financial Analysts Journal 67, No. 1 (2011): 40-54. https://doi.org/10.2469/faj.v67.n1.4.

Baker, Malcolm, and Jeffrey Wurgler. "Investor Sentiment in the Stock Market." The Journal of Economic Perspectives 21, No. 2 (2007): 129–51. http://www.jstor.org/stable/30033721.

Bali, Turan G., Lin Peng, Yannan Shen, and Yi Tang. "Liquidity Shocks and Stock Market Reactions." The Review of Financial Studies 27, No. 5 (2014): 1434–1485. https://doi.org/10.1093/rfs/hht074.

Ball, Ray, and Philip Brown. "An Empirical Evaluation of Accounting Income Numbers." Journal of Accounting Research 6, No. 2 (1968): 159–78. https://doi.org/10.2307/2490232.

Baltussen, Guido. "Behavioral Finance: An Introduction." SSRN Electronic Journal (January 13, 2009). https://dx.doi.org/10.2139/ssrn.1488110.

Banz, Rolf W. "The Relation between Return and Market Value of Common Stocks." Journal of Financial Economics 9, No. 1 (1981): 3−18. https://doi.org/10.1016/0304-405X(81)90018-0.

Barber, Brad. M., Yi-Tsung Lee, Yu-Jane Liu, and Terrance Odean. "The Cross-section of Speculator Skill: Evidence from Day Trading." Journal of Financial Markets 18, No. 1 (2014): 1-24. http://doi.org/10.1016/j.finmar.2013.05.006.

Barber, Brad. M., and Terrance Odean. "All that Glitters: The Effect of Attention on the Buying Behavior of Individual and Institutional Investors." The Review of Financial Studies 21, No. 2 (2008): 785-818. https://doi.org/10.1093/rfs/hhm079.

Barber, Brad M., and Terrance Odean. "The Behavior of Individual Investors." In Handbook of the Economics of Finance, edited by George M. Constantinides, Milton Harris, and René M. Stulz, Vol. 2, part B, 1533–1570. (Amsterdam: North-Holland, 2013).

Barber, Brad M., Terrance Odean, and Ning Zhu. "Systematic Noise." Journal of Financial Markets 12, No. 4 (2009): 547-569. https://doi.org/10.1016/j.finmar.2009.03.003.

Barberis, Nicholas, Robin Greenwood, Lawrence Jin, and Andrei Shleifer. "Extrapolation and Bubbles." Journal of Financial Economics 129, No. 2 (2018): 203-227.

https://doi.org/10.1016/j.jfineco.2018.04.007.

Barberis, Nicholas, and Ming Huang. "Mental Accounting, Loss Aversion, and Individual Stock Returns." The Journal of Finance 56, No. 4 (2001): 1247–92.
https://doi.org/10.1111/0022-1082.00367.

Barberis, Nicholas, and Andrei Shleifer. "Style Investing." Journal of Financial Economics 68, No. 2 (2003): 161-199.
https://doi.org/10.1016/S0304-405X(03)00064-3.

Barberis, Nicholas, Andrei Shleifer, and Robert Vishny. "A Model of Investor Sentiment." Journal of Financial Economics 49, No. 3 (1998): 307-343.
https://doi.org/10.1016/S0304-405X(98)00027-0.

Barberis, Nicholas and Richard Thaler. "A Survey of Behavioral Finance." In Handbook of the Economics of Finance, edited by George M. Constantinides, Milton Harris, and René M. Stulz, Volume 1, part B, 1053-1128. (Amsterdam: North-Holland, 2003).

Barberis, Nicholas, and Wei Xiong. "Realization Utility." Journal of Financial Economics 104, No. 2 (2012): 251-271.
https://doi.org/10.1016/j.jfineco.2011.10.005.

Bartlett, Robert P., Justin McCrary, and Maureen O'Hara. "Tiny Trades, Big Questions: Fractional Shares." SSRN Electronic Journal (October 14, 2022).
http://dx.doi.org/10.2139/ssrn.4248449.

Bartram, Söhnke M., Harald Lohre, Peter F. Pope, and Ananthalakshmi Ranganathan. "Navigating the Factor Zoo around the World: An Institutional Investor Perspective." The Journal of Business Economics 91 (2021): 655–703.
https://doi.org/10.1007/s11573-021-01035-y.

Bee, Michele, and Maxime Desmarais-Tremblay. "The Birth of Homo Œconomicus: The Methodological Debate on the Economic Agent from J. S. Mill to V. Pareto." Journal of the History of Economic Thought 45, No. 1 (2023): 1–26.
https://doi.org/10.1017/S1053837221000535.

Bell, Adrian R., Chris Brooks, and Nick Taylor. "Time-varying Price Discovery in the Eighteenth Century: Empirical Evidence from the London and Amsterdam Stock Markets." Cliometrica 10 (2016): 5–30.
https://doi.org/10.1007/s11698-014-0120-z.

ben Maimon ("Maimonides"), Rabbi Moshe. "Klei Hamikdash", Chapter 6:1. Sefer Avodah-Mishneh Torah. Accessed May 25, 2024.
https://www.chabad.org/library/article_cdo/aid/1008231/jewish/Klei-m-Chapter-6.htm.

ben Maimon ("Maimonides"), Rabbi Moshe. "Ma'aser Sheni", Chapter 4:21. Sefer Zeraim. Accessed May 25, 2024. https://www.chabad.org/library/article_cdo/aid/997089/jewish/Maaser-Sheini-Chapter-4.htm.

Benartzi, Shlomo, and Richard H. Thaler. "Myopic Loss Aversion and the Equity Premium Puzzle." The Quarterly Journal of Economics 110, No. 1 (1995): 73–92. https://doi.org/10.2307/2118511.

Berger, Shlomo. "Ashkenazim Read Sephardim in Seventeenth- and Eighteenth-Century Amsterdam." Studia Rosenthaliana 35, No. 2 (2001): 253–65. http://www.jstor.org/stable/41482457.

Biale, David. 2012. Cultures of the Jews: A New History. New York: Knopf Doubleday Publishing Group.

Black, Fisher. "Noise." The Journal of Finance 41, No. 3 (1986): 529-543. https://doi.org/10.1111/j.1540-6261.1986.tb04513.x.

Bohl, Martin T., Carsten Burhop, Arne C. Klein, and Pierre L. Siklos. "Herding During the German Hyperinflation." Working paper, Department of Economics, Westphalian Wilhelminian University of Münster (March, 2012).

Brav, Alon, and J. B. Heaton. "Competing Theories of Financial Anomalies." The Review of Financial Studies 15, No. 2 (2002): 575–606. https://doi.org/10.1093/rfs/15.2.575.

Brogaard, Jonathan, Thanh Huong Nguyen, Talis J Putnins, and Eliza Wu. "What Moves Stock Prices? The Roles of News, Noise, and Information." The Review of Financial Studies 35, No. 9 (2022): 4341–4386. https://doi.org/10.1093/rfs/hhab137.

Brunnermeier, Markus K. "Bubbles." In New Palgrave Dictionary of Economics, edited by Matias Vernengo, Esteban Perez Caldentey and Barkley J. Rosser Jr. (2nd ed.), 1-8. (London: Palgrave Macmillan, 2008).

Brunnermeier, Markus K., and John Morgan. "Clock Games: Theory and Experiments." Games and Economic Behavior 68, No. 2 (2010): 532-550. https://doi.org/10.1016/j.geb.2009.09.005.

Bryzgalova, Svetlana, Jiantao Huang, and Christian Julliard. "Bayesian Solutions for the Factor Zoo: We Just Ran Two Quadrillion Models." The Journal of Finance 78, No. 1 (2023): 487-557. https://doi.org/10.1111/jofi.13197.

Burt, Roger. "Freemasonry and Business Networking during the Victorian Period." The Economic History Review 56, No. 4 (2003): 657-688. https://doi.org/10.1111/j.1468-0289.2003.00265.x

Camerer, Colin F., George Loewenstein, and Drazen Prelec. "Neuroeconomics: Why Economics Needs Brains." Scandinavian Journal of Economics 106, No. 3 (2004): 555-579. https://doi.org/10.1111/j.0347-0520.2004.00377.x.

Camerer, Colin F., George Loewenstein, and Drazen Prelec. "Neuroeconomics: How Neuroscience can Inform Economics." Journal of Economic Literature 43, No. 1 (2005): 9–64. https://doi.org/10.1257/0022051053737843.

Cardoso, José Luís. "*Confusion de confusions*: ethics and options on seventeenth-century stock exchange markets." Financial History Review 9, No. 2 (2002): 109-123. https://doi.org/10.1017/S0968565002000100.

Carlin, Bruce I., Francis A. Longstaff, and Kyle Matoba. "Disagreement and Asset Prices." Journal of Financial Economics 114, No. 2 (2014): 226-238. https://doi.org/10.1016/j.jfineco.2014.06.007.

Chang, Tom Y., David H. Solomon, and Mark M. Westerfield. "Looking for Someone to Blame: Delegation, Cognitive Dissonance, and the Disposition Effect." The Journal of Finance 71, No. 1 (2016): 267–302. https://doi.org/10.1111/jofi.12311.

Chau, Frankie, Rataporn Deesomsak, and Dimitrios Koutmos. "Does Investor Sentiment Really Matter?" International Review of Financial Analysis 48 (2016): 221-232. https://doi.org/10.1016/j.irfa.2016.10.003.

Chelley-Steeley, Patricia, Neophytos Lambertides, and Christos S. Savva. "Sentiment, Order Imbalance, and Co-movement: An Examination of Shocks to Retail and Institutional Trading Activity." European Financial Management 25, No. 1 (2019): 116–159. https://doi.org/10.1111/eufm.12146.

Ch'eng-en, Wu. 1973. Monkey. London: Penguin Classics.

Chen, Chun-nan, and Chunchi Wu. "Small Trades and Volatility Increases after Stock Splits." International Review of Economics & Finance 18, No. 4 (2009): 592-610. https://doi.org/10.1016/j.iref.2008.10.005.

Chiarella, Carl, Xue-Zhong He, and Remco C.J. Zwinkels. "Heterogeneous Expectations in Asset Pricing: Empirical Evidence from the S&P500." Journal of Economic Behavior and Organization 105 (2014): 1-16. https://doi.org/10.1016/j.jebo.2014.03.003.

Clason, George, S. 1926. The Richest Man in Babylon. Reader's Library Classics.

Cochrane, John H. "Presidential Address: Discount Rates." The Journal of Finance 66, No. 4 (2011): 1047-1108. https://doi.org/10.1111/j.1540-6261.2011.01671.x.

Cookson, J. Anthony, Vyacheslav Fos, and Marina Niessner. "Does Disagreement Facilitate Informed Trading?" SSRN Electronic Journal (September 27, 2022). https://dx.doi.org/10.2139/ssrn.3765092.

Corzo, Teresa, Margarita Prat, and Esther Vaquero. "Behavioral Finance in Joseph de la Vega's Confusion de Confusiones." Journal of Behavioral Finance 15, No. 4 (2014): 341-350. https://doi.org/10.1080/15427560.2014.968722.

Crépellière, Tommy, Matthias Pelster, and Stefan Zeisberger. "Arbitrage in the Market for Cryptocurrencies." Journal of Financial Markets 64 (2023): 100817. https://doi.org/10.1016/j.finmar.2023.100817.

Da, Zhi, Vivian W. Fang, and Wenwei Lin. "Fractional Trading." SSRN Electronic Journal (November 18, 2021). https://dx.doi.org/10.2139/ssrn.3949697.

Dai, Min, Yipeng Jiang, Hong Liu, and Jing Xu. "A Rational Theory for Disposition Effects." Review of Economic Dynamics 47 (2023): 131-157. https://doi.org/10.1016/j.red.2021.11.003.

Davidi, Einat. "The Corpus of Hebrew and Jewish *Autos Sacramentales*: Self-deception and Conversion." European Journal of Jewish Studies 13 (2019a):182–226. http://dx.doi.org/10.1163/1872471X-11211064.

Davidi, Einat. "Penso de la Vega and the Question of Jewish Baroque." In Religious Changes and Cultural Transformations in the Early Modern Western Sephardic Communities, edited by Yosef Kaplan (1st ed.), 469-483. (Leiden; Boston: Brill, 2019b).

Dávila, Eduardo, Daniel D. Graves, and Cecilia Parlatore. "The Value of Arbitrage." *National Bureau of Economic Research Working Paper 29744*, (February 2022).

De Bondt, Werner F. M., and Richard Thaler. "Does the Stock Market Overreact?" The Journal of Finance 40, No. 3 (1985): 793–805. https://doi.org/10.2307/2327804.

De Bondt, Werner F. M., and Richard H. Thaler. "Further Evidence on Investor Overreaction and Stock Market Seasonality." The Journal of Finance 42, No. 3 (1987): 557–81.

https://doi.org/10.2307/2328371.

De Jong, Abe, Leonard Rosenthal, and Mathijs A. Van Dijk. "The Risk and Return of Arbitrage in Dual-Listed Companies." Review of Finance 13, No. 3 (2009): 495–520. https://doi.org/10.1093/rof/rfn031.

De la Vega, Joseph Penso. 1957. Confusion de Confusiones, 1688: Portions Descriptive of the Amsterdam Stock Exchange (No. 13). Boston: Baker Library, Harvard Graduate School of Business Administration.

De Long, J. Bradford, Andrei Shleifer, Lawrence H. Summers, and Robert J. Waldmann. "Positive Feedback Investment Strategies and Destabilizing Rational Speculation." The Journal of Finance 45, No. 2 (1990a): 379–95. https://doi.org/10.2307/2328662.

De Long, J. Bradford, Andrei Shleifer, Lawrence H. Summers, and Robert J. Waldmann. "Noise Trader Risk in Financial Markets." Journal of Political Economy 98, No. 4 (1990b): 703–38. https://doi.org/10.1086/261703.

De Marchi, Neil, and Paul Harrison. "Trading "in the Wind" and with Guile: The Troublesome Matter of the Short-selling of Shares in Seventeenth-century Holland." History of Political Economy, Supplement, 26, No. 0 (1994), 47–65. https://doi.org/10.1215/00182702-1994-suppl_1008.

Dempster, Greg., John M. Wells and Douglas T. Wills. "A Common-Features Analysis of Amsterdam and London Financial Markets during the Eighteenth Century." Economic Inquiry 38, No. 1 (2000): 19-33. https://doi.org/10.1111/j.1465-7295.2000.tb00002.x.

Deschamps, Simon. "Merchant and Masonic Networks in Eighteenth-Century Colonial India." XVII-XVIII 74 (2017a). https://doi.org/10.4000/1718.828

Deschamps, Simon. "From Britain to India: Freemasonry as a Connective Force of Empire." e-Rea 14, No. 2 (2017b). https://doi.org/10.4000/erea.5853

Desmoulins-Lebeault, François, Jean-François Gajewski, and Luc Meunier. "What can we Learn from Neurofinance?" Finance 39, No. 2 (2018): 93-148. https://doi.org/10.3917/fina.392.0093.

Devault, Luke, Richard Sias, and Laura Starks. "Sentiment Metrics and Investor Demand." The Journal of Finance 74, No. 2 (2019): 985–1024. https://doi.org/10.1111/jofi.12754.

Devenow, Andrea, and Ivo Welch. "Rational Herding in Financial Economics." European Economic Review 40, No 3-5 (1996): 603–615.

https://doi.org/10.1016/0014-2921(95)00073-9.

Ding, Rong, and Wenxuan Hou. "Retail Investor Attention and Stock Liquidity." Journal of International Financial Markets, Institutions and Money 37 (2015):12–26. https://doi.org/10.1016/j.intfin.2015.04.001

Dorn, Daniel, Gur Huberman, and Paul Sengmueller. "Correlated Trading and Returns." The Journal of Finance 63, No. 2 (2008): 885–920. https://doi.org/10.1111/j.1540-6261.2008.01334.x.

Dumez, Hervé. "The Description of the first Financial Market: Looking Back on Confusion of Confusions by Joseph de la Vega." Annales des Mines-Gérer et comprendre 1, No. 119 (2015): 7-12. https://doi.org/10.3917/geco1.119.0007.

Duong, Huu Nhan, Abhinav Goyal, Vasileios Kallinterakis, and Madhu Veeraraghavan. "Democracy and the Pricing of Initial Public Offerings around the World." Journal of Financial Economics 145, No. 1 (2022): 322-341. https://doi.org/10.1016/j.jfineco.2021.07.010

Dweck, Yaacob. "Jacob Sasportas and Problems of Discipline in the Ets Haim Yeshiva." In Religious Changes and Cultural Transformations in the Early Modern Western Sephardic Communities, edited by Yosef Kaplan (1st ed.), 383-392. (Leiden; Boston: Brill, 2019).

Dzieliński, Michał, Marc Oliver Rieger, and Tõnn Talpsepp. "Asymmetric Attention and Volatility Asymmetry." Journal of Empirical Finance 45 (2018):59–67. https://doi.org/10.1016/j.jempfin.2017.09.010.

Economou, Fotini, Konstantinos Gavriilidis, Bartosz Gebka, and Vasileios Kallinterakis. "Feedback Trading: A Review of Theory and Empirical Evidence." Review of Behavioral Finance 15, No. 4 (2023): 429-476. https://doi.org/10.1108/RBF-12-2021-0268.

Ecclesiastes 1:9-11, In King James Bible. (Glasgow: Collins, 2016).

Edwards, Ward. "Conservatism in Human Information Processing." In Judgment under Uncertainty: Heuristics and Biases, edited by Daniel Kahneman, Paul Slovic, and Amos Tversky, 359–69. (Cambridge: Cambridge University Press, 1982).

Elkind, Daniel, Kathryn Kaminski, Andrew W. Lo, Kien Wei Siah, and Chi Heem Wong. "When do Investors freak out? Machine Learning Predictions of Panic Selling." Journal of Financial Data Science 4, No. 1 (2022): 11–39. https://doi.org/10.3905/jfds.2021.1.085.

Fama, Eugene F. "The Behavior of Stock-Market Prices." The Journal of Business 38, No. 1 (1965): 34–105.

https://doi.org/10.1086/294743.

Fama, Eugene F. "Efficient Capital Markets: A Review of Theory and Empirical Work." The Journal of Finance 25, No. 2 (1970): 383–417. https://doi.org/10.2307/2325486.

Fama, Eugene F. "Efficient Capital Markets: II." The Journal of Finance 46, No. 5 (1991): 1575–1617. https://doi.org/10.2307/2328565.

Fama, Eugene F. "Market Efficiency, Long-Term Returns, and Behavioral Finance." Journal of Financial Economics 49, No. 3 (1998): 283-306. https://doi.org/10.1016/S0304-405X(98)00026-9.

Fama, Eugene F., Lawrence Fisher, Michael C. Jensen, and Richard Roll. "The Adjustment of Stock Prices to New Information." International Economic Review 10, No. 1 (1969): 1–21. https://doi.org/10.2307/2525569.

Fama, Eugene F., and Marshall E. Blume. "Filter Rules and Stock-Market Trading." The Journal of Business 39, No. 1 (1966): 226–41. https://doi.org/10.1086/294849.

Farmer, Jay Doyne. "Market Force, Ecology and Evolution." Industrial and Corporate Change 11, No. 5 (2002): 895-953. https://doi.org/10.1093/icc/11.5.895.

Feng, Guanhao, Stefano Giglio, and Dacheng Xiu. "Taming the Factor Zoo: A Test of New Factors." The Journal of Finance 75, No. 3 (2020): 1327-1370. https://doi.org/10.1111/jofi.12883.

Frazzini, Andrea, and Owen A. Lamont. "Dumb Money: Mutual Fund Flows and the Cross-section of Stock Returns." Journal of Financial Economics 88, No. 2 (2008): 99–322. https://doi.org/10.1016/j.jfineco.2007.07.001.

Friedman, Milton. 1953. Essays in Positive Economics. Chicago: University of Chicago Press.

Frijns, Bart, and Remco C.J. Zwinkels. "Absence of Speculation in the European Sovereign Debt Markets." Journal of Economic Behavior and Organization 169 (2020): 245-265. https://doi.org/10.1016/j.jebo.2019.11.017.

Froot, Kenneth A., and Emil M. Dabora. "How are Stock Prices Affected by the Location of Trade?" Journal of Financial Economics 53, No. 2 (1999):189–216. https://doi.org/10.1016/S0304-405X(99)00020-3.

Galariotis, Emilios. "Contrarian and Momentum Trading: A Review of the Literature." Review of Behavioral Finance 6, No. 1 (2014): 63-82. https://doi.org/10.1108/RBF-12-2013-0043.

Galbraith, John Kenneth. 1994. A Short History of Economic Euphoria. London: Penguin Books.

Gallant, A. Ronald, Peter E. Rossi, and George Tauchen. "Stock Prices and Volume." The Review of Financial Studies 5, No. 2 (1992): 199–242. https://doi.org/10.1093/rfs/5.2.199.

Gampel, Benjamin R. "Jews, Christians, and Muslims in Medieval Iberia: Convivencia through the Eyes of Sephardic Jews." In Convivencia: Jews, Muslims, and Christians in Medieval Spain, edited by Vivian B. Mann, Thomas F. Glick, and Jerrilynn D. Dodds, 11-37. (New York: George Braziller, Inc, 1992).

Gavriilidis, Konstantinos, and Vasileios Kallinterakis. "Herding in Imperial Russia: Evidence from the St. Petersburg Stock Exchange (1865–1914)." Journal of Behavioral Finance 24, No. 4 (2023): 383-397. https://doi.org/10.1080/15427560.2021.1986715.

Geanakoplos, John D., and Heraklis M. Polemarchakis. "We Can't Disagree Forever." Journal of Economic Theory 28, No. 1 (1982): 192–200. https://doi.org/10.1016/0022-0531(82)90099-0.

Geczy, Christopher C., and Mikhail Samonov. "Two Centuries of Price-return Momentum." Financial Analysts Journal 72, No. 5 (2016): 32–56.
https://doi.org/10.2469/faj.v72.n5.1.

Gelderblom, Oscar, Abe de Jong, and Joost Jonker. "An Admiralty for Asia. Isaac le Maire and Conflicting Conceptions About the Corporate Governance of the VOC." In The Origins of Shareholder Advocacy, edited by Jonathan G. S. Koppell, 29-60. (New York: Palgrave Macmillan, 2011).

Gelderblom, Oscar, Abe de Jong, and Joost Jonker. "The Formative Years of the Modern Corporation: The Dutch East India Company VOC, 1602–1623." The Journal of Economic History 73, No. 4 (2013): 1050–1076. https://doi.org/10.1017/S0022050713000879.

Gelderblom, Oscar, and Joost Jonker. "Completing a Financial Revolution: The Finance of the Dutch East India Trade and the Rise of the Amsterdam Capital Market, 1595-1612." The Journal of Economic History 64, No. 3 (2004): 641–72.
https://doi.org/10.1017/S002205070400292X.

Gennaioli, Nicola, Andrei Shleifer, and Robert Vishny. "Neglected Risks: The Psychology of Financial Crises." American Economic Review, 105, No. 5 (2015): 310-14.
https://doi.org/10.1257/AER.P20151091.

Gerding, Erik F. "The Next Epidemic: Bubbles and the Growth and Decay of Securities Regulation." Connecticut Law Review, 38 (2006): 393-453.

Gernandt, Otto, Thomas Palm, and Daniel Waldenström. "Liquidity Premia During the Industrial Breakthrough: Evidence from the Stockholm Stock Exchange, 1901-1919." European Review of Economic History 16, No. 3 (2012): 247-269. https://doi.org/10.1093/ereh/hes002.

Gervais, Simon, Kaniel, Ron, and Dan H. Mingelgrin. "The High Volume Return Premium." The Journal of Finance 56, No. 3 (2001): 877-919. https://doi.org/10.1111/0022-1082.00349.

Goetzmann, William N., and Simon Huang. "Momentum in Imperial Russia." Journal of Financial Economics 130, No. 3 (2018): 579-591. https://doi.org/10.1016/j.jfineco.2018.07.008.

Goetzmann, William N., Roger G. Ibbotson, and Liang Peng. "A New Historical Database for the NYSE 1815 to 1925: Performance and Predictability." Journal of Financial Markets 4, No. 1 (2001): 1-32. https://doi.org/10.1016/S1386-4181(00)00013-6.

Goetzmann, William Nelson, and Nadav Peles. "Cognitive Dissonance and Mutual Fund Investors." Journal of Financial Research 20, No. 2 (1997): 145-158. https://doi.org/10.1111/j.1475-6803.1997.tb00241.x.

Goldish, Matt. "The Amsterdam Portuguese Rabbinate in the Seventeenth Century: A Unique Institution Viewed from Within and Without." In Dutch Jews as Perceived by Themselves and by Others (Proceedings of the Eighth International Symposium on the History of the Jews in the Netherlands) edited by Chaya Brasz and Yosef Kaplan, 9-19. (Leiden: Brill, 2001).

Griffin, John M., and Amin Shams. "Is Bitcoin Really Untethered?" The Journal of Finance 75, No. 4 (2020): 1913-1964. https://doi.org/10.1111/jofi.12903.

Grossman, Sanford J., and Joseph E. Stiglitz. "On the Impossibility of Informationally Efficient Markets." The American Economic Review 70, No. 3 (1980): 393–408. https://doi.org/10.7916/D8765R99.

Gujarati, Damodar N. 2003. Basic Econometrics. New York: McGraw-Hill/Irwin.

Gutiérrez-Nieto, Begoña, Cristina Ortiz, and Luis Vicente. "A Bibliometric Analysis of the Disposition Effect: Origins and Future Research Avenues." Journal of Behavioral and Experimental Finance 37 (2023), 100774.

https://doi.org/10.1016/j.jbef.2022.100774.

Harmon-Jones, Eddie, and Judson Mills. "An Introduction to Cognitive Dissonance Theory and an Overview of Current Perspectives on the Theory." In Cognitive Dissonance: Reexamining a Pivotal Theory in Psychology edited by Eddie Harmon-Jones (2nd ed.), 3–24. (Washington, DC: American Psychological Association, 2019). https://doi.org/10.1037/0000135-001

Hart, William, Dolores Albarracín, Alice H. Eagly, Inge Brechan, Matthew J Lindberg, and Lisa Merrill. "Feeling Validated Versus Being Correct: A Meta-analysis of Selective Exposure to Information." Psychological Bulletin 135, No. 4 (2009): 555-88. https://doi.org/10.1037/a0015701.

Harvey, Campbell R. and Yan Liu. "A Census of the Factor Zoo". SSRN Electronic Journal (February 25, 2019). https://dx.doi.org/10.2139/ssrn.3341728.

Harvey, Campbell R., Yan Liu, and Heqing Zhu. "...And the Cross-Section of Expected Returns." The Review of Financial Studies 29, No. 1 (2016): 5–68. https://doi.org/10.1093/rfs/hhv059.

He, Xue-Zhong, and Huanhuan Zheng. "Trading Heterogeneity under Information Uncertainty." Journal of Economic Behavior and Organization, *130 (2016): 64-80.* https://doi.org/10.1016/j.jebo.2016.07.001.

Heertje, Arnold. "Jewish Background." In The Elgar Companion to David Ricardo, edited by Heinz D. Kurz and Neri Salvadori, 217-224. (Cheltenham: Edward Elgar Publishing, 2015).

Held, Paul. "*The Confusion of Confusions*: Between Speculation and Eschatology." Concentric: Literary and Cultural Studies 32, No. 2 (2006): 111-145.

Hirshleifer, David. "Investor Psychology and Asset Pricing." The Journal of Finance 56, No. 4 (2001): 1533-1598. https://doi.org/10.1111/0022-1082.00379.

Hirshleifer, David. "Psychological Bias as a Driver of Financial Regulation." European Financial Management 14, No. 5 (2008): 856-874. https://doi.org/10.1111/j.1468-036X.2007.00437.x.

Hirshleifer, David. "Behavioral Finance." Annual Review of Financial Economics, 7 (2015): 133-159. https://doi.org/10.1146/annurev-financial-092214-043752.

Hirshleifer, David, Avanidhar Subrahmanyam, and Sheridan Titman. "Security Analysis and Trading Patterns When Some Investors Receive

Information before Others." The Journal of Finance 49, No. 5 (1994): 1665–98.
https://doi.org/10.1111/j.1540-6261.1994.tb04777.x.

Hirshleifer, David. and Siew Hong Teoh. "Herd Behavior and Cascading in Capital Markets: A Review and Synthesis." European Financial Management 9, No. 1 (2003): 25-66.
https://doi.org/10.1111/1468-036X.00207.

Hirshleifer, David, and Ivo Welch. "An Economic Approach to the Psychology of Change: Amnesia, Inertia, and Impulsiveness." Journal of Economics & Management Strategy 11, No. 3 (2002): 379-421.
https://doi.org/10.1111/j.1430-9134.2002.00379.x.

Hoffmann, Arvid O.I., and Hersh Shefrin. "Technical Analysis and Individual Investors." Journal of Economic Behavior & Organization 107, Part B (2014): 487-511.
https://doi.org/10.1016/j.jebo.2014.04.002

Holmes, Phil, Vasileios Kallinterakis, and Mario Pedro Leite-Ferreira. "Herding in a Concentrated Market: A Question of Intent." European Financial Management 19, No. 3 (2013): 497–520.
https://doi.org/10.1111/j.1468-036X.2010.00592.x.

Hou, Kewei, Chen Xue, and Lu Zhang. "Replicating Anomalies." The Review of Financial Studies 33, No. 5 (2020): 2019–2133.
https://doi.org/10.1093/rfs/hhy131.

Hung, Weifeng, Ching-Ting Lin, and J. Jimmy Yang. "Aggregate 52-week High, Limited Attention, and time-varying Momentum Profits." Journal of Financial Economics 141 (2022): 106531.
https://doi.org/10.1016/j.jbankfin.2022.106531.

Hwang, Soosung, and Mark Salmon. "Market Stress and Herding." Journal of Empirical Finance 11, No. 4 (2004): 585–616.
https://doi.org/10.1016/j.jempfin.2004.04.003.

Israel, Jonathan. "Spain and the Dutch Sephardim, 1609-1660." Studia Rosenthaliana 12, No. 1/2 (1978): 1–61.
http://www.jstor.org/stable/41481273.

Israel, Jonathan. "Some further Data on the Amsterdam Sephardim and their Trade with Spain during the 1650s." Studia Rosenthaliana 14, No. 1 (1980): 7–19.
http://www.jstor.org/stable/41481325.

Israel, Jonathan. "Sephardic Immigration into the Dutch Republic, 1595-1672." Studia Rosenthaliana 23 (1989): 45–53.
http://www.jstor.org/stable/41481727.

Israel, Jonathan. 1995. The Dutch Republic: Its rise, greatness, and fall, 1477–1806. Oxford: Oxford University Press.

Israeli, Doron, Ron Kaniel, and Suhas A. Sridharan. "The Real Side of the High-Volume Return Premium." Management Science 68, No. 2 (2021): 1426-1449. https://doi.org/10.1287/mnsc.2020.3886

Jansen, Jan C. "In Search of Atlantic Sociability: Freemasons, Empires, and Atlantic History." Bulletin of the German Historical Institute 57 (2015): 75–99.

Jegadeesh, Narasimhan, and Sheridan Titman. "Returns to Buying Winners and Selling Losers: Implications for Stock Market Efficiency." The Journal of Finance 48, No. 1 (1993): 65–91. https://doi.org/10.2307/2328882.

Jensen, Michael C. "The Performance of Mutual Funds in the Period 1945-64." The Journal of Finance, 23, No. 2 (1968): 389-416. https://doi.org/10.1111/j.1540-6261.1968.tb00815.x

Jensen, Michael C. "Some Anomalous Evidence Regarding Market Efficiency." Journal of Financial Economics 6, No. 2–3 (1978): 95-101. https://doi.org/10.1016/0304-405X(78)90025-9.

Jones, Charles M., Gautam Kaul, and Marc L. Lipson. "Transactions, Volume, and Volatility." The Review of Financial Studies 7, No. 4 (1994): 631–51. https://doi.org/10.1093/rfs/7.4.631.

Jonker, Joost, and Keetie Sluyterman. 2000. At Home on the World Markets: Dutch International Trading Companies from the 16th Century until the Present. The Hague: SDU Uitgevers.

Josephus, Flavius. 1981. The Jewish War. London: Penguin Classics.

Josephus, Flavius. 2023. The Antiquities of the Jews. United Kingdom: Moncreiffe Press.

Jovanovic, Franck, and Philippe Le Gall. "Does God practice a Random Walk? The "Financial Physics" of a 19th Century Forerunner, Jules Regnault." European Journal of the History of Economic Thought 8, No. 3 (2018): 332-362. https://doi.org/10.1080/09672560110062960

Kahneman, Daniel. 2012. Thinking, Fast and Slow. London: Penguin Books.

Kahneman, Daniel, and Shane Frederick. "Representativeness Revisited: Attribute Substitution in Intuitive Judgment." In Heuristics and Biases: The Psychology of Intuitive Judgment, edited by Thomas Gilovic, Dale Griffin and Daniel Kahneman, 49-81. (New York: Cambridge University Press, 2002).

Kahneman, Daniel, Jack L. Knetsch, and Richard H. Thaler. “Experimental Tests of the Endowment Effect and the Coase Theorem.” Journal of Political Economy, 98, No. 6 (1990): 1325-1348. https://doi.org/10.1086/261737.

Kahneman, Daniel, and Amos Tversky. “Subjective Probability: A Judgment of Representativeness.” Cognitive Psychology 3, No. 3 (1972): 430–454. https://doi.org/10.1016/0010-0285(72)90016-3.

Kahneman, Daniel, and Amos Tversky. “Prospect Theory: An Analysis of Decision under Risk.” Econometrica 47, No. 2 (1979): 263–91. https://doi.org/10.2307/1914185.

Kallinterakis, Vasileios and Greg N. Gregoriou. “Herd Behaviour: A Survey.” AESTIMATIO, The IEB Journal of Finance, 14 (2017): 8-25. http://www.ieb.es/wp-content/uploads/2016/06/Aestimatio/0.pdf.

Kamara, Avraham, and Jennifer Lynch Koski. “Volatility, Autocorrelations, and Trading Activity after Stock Splits.” Journal of Financial Markets 4, No. 2 (2001): 163-184. https://doi.org/10.1016/S1386-4181(00)00018-5.

Kaniel, Ron, Arzu Ozoguz, and Laura Starks. “The High Volume Return Premium: Cross Country Evidence.” Journal of Financial Economics 103, No. 2 (2012): 255-279. https://doi.org/10.1016/j.jfineco.2011.08.012.

Kaplan, Yosef. “The Portuguese Jews in Amsterdam. From Forced Conversion to a Return to Judaism.” Studia Rosenthaliana 15, No. 1 (1981): 37–51. http://www.jstor.org/stable/41481884.

Kaplan, Yosef. “Amsterdam and Ashkenazic Migration in the Seventeenth Century.” Studia Rosenthaliana 23 (1989): 22–44. http://www.jstor.org/stable/41481726.

Karpoff, Jonathan M. “The Relation Between Price Changes and Trading Volume: A Survey.” The Journal of Financial and Quantitative Analysis 22, No. 1 (1987): 109–26. https://doi.org/10.2307/2330874.

Kaustia, Markku, & Samuli Knüpfer. “Do Investors Overweight Personal Experience? Evidence from IPO Subscriptions.” The Journal of Finance 63, No. 6 (2008): 2679-2702. https://doi.org/10.1111/j.1540-6261.2008.01411.x.

Keown, Arthur J., and John M. Pinkerton. “Merger Announcements and Insider Trading Activity: An Empirical Investigation.” The Journal of Finance 36, No. 4 (1981): 855–69. https://doi.org/10.2307/2327551.

Khwaja, Asim Ijaz and Atif Mian. "Unchecked Intermediaries: Price Manipulation in an Emerging Stock Market." Journal of Financial Economics 78, No. 1 (2005): 203-241. https://doi.org/10.1016/j.jfineco.2004.06.014.

Kindleberger, Charles. P. and Robert Z. Aliber. 2005. Manias, Panics and Crashes. New Jersey: John Wiley & Sons.

Klooster, Wim. "Sephardic Migration and the Growth of European Long-Distance Trade." Studia Rosenthaliana 35, No. 2 (2001): 121–32. http://www.jstor.org/stable/41482448.

Koen, E.M. "The Earliest Sources Relating to the Portuguese Jews in the Municipal Archives of Amsterdam up to 1620." Studia Rosenthaliana 4, No. 1 (1970): 25–42. http://www.jstor.org/stable/41481360.

Konnikova, Maria. 2013. Mastermind: How to think like Sherlock Holmes. Edinburgh: Canongate Books Ltd.

Kroon, Andréa A. 2015. Masonic Networks, Material Culture and International Trade: The Participation of Dutch Freemasons in the Commercial and Cultural Exchange with Southeast Asia (1735-1853). Doctoral thesis, Leiden University Centre for the Arts in Society (LUCAS), Geesteswetenschappen, Leiden University, Netherlands. https://hdl.handle.net/1887/36561

Kumar, Alok. "Hard-to-value Stocks, Behavioral Biases, and Informed Trading." Journal of Financial and Quantitative Analysis 44, No. 6 (2009): 1375-1401. https://doi.org/10.1017/S0022109009990342.

Kumar, Praveen, and Duane J. Seppi. "Futures Manipulation with 'Cash Settlement.'" The Journal of Finance 47, No. 4 (1992): 1485–1502. https://doi.org/10.2307/2328948.

Lakonishok, Josef, Andrei Shleifer, and Robert W. Vishny. "Contrarian Investment, Extrapolation, and Risk." The Journal of Finance 49, No. 5 (1994): 1541–78. https://doi.org/10.2307/2329262.

Lakonishok, Josef, and Seymour Smidt. "Are Seasonal Anomalies Real? A Ninety-Year Perspective." The Review of Financial Studies 1, No. 4 (1988): 403–25. https://doi.org/10.1093/rfs/1.4.403.

Lehmann-Hasemeyer, Sibylle, and Alexander Opitz. "Data Sources on the 19th and Early 20th Century German Capital Market: Challenges and Opportunities." German Economic Review (2024). https://doi.org/10.1515/ger-2024-0067

LeRoy, Stephen F., and Richard D. Porter. "The Present-Value Relation: Tests Based on Implied Variance Bounds." Econometrica 49, No. 3 (1981): 555–74.
https://doi.org/10.2307/1911512.

Leung, Henry, Tse-Chun Lin, and Ruiqi Mao. "Alternative Stars: Do Key Opinion Leaders on Social Media Move the Market?" SSRN Electronic Journal (November 10, 2022).
https://dx.doi.org/10.2139/ssrn.4273951.

Leuz, Christian, Steffen Meyer, Maximilian Muhn, Eugene F. Soltes, and Andreas Hackethal. "Who Falls Prey to the Wolf of Wall Street? Investor Participation in Market Manipulation." SSRN Electronic Journal (September 30, 2023).
https://dx.doi.org/10.2139/ssrn.3073817.

Liao, Tsai-Ling, Chih-Jen Huang, and Chieh-Yuan Wu. "Do Fund Managers Herd to Counter Investor Sentiment?" The Journal of Business Research 64, No. 2 (2011): 207-212.
https://doi.org/10.1016/j.jbusres.2010.01.007.

Lo, Andrew W., and A. Craig MacKinlay. 1999. A Non-Random Walk Down Wall Street. New Jersey: Princeton University Press.

Lo, Andrew.W., Harry Mamaysky, and Jiang Wang. "Foundations of Technical Analysis: Computational Algorithms, Statistical Inference, and Empirical Implementation." Journal of Finance 55 No. 4 (2000): 1705-1770.
https://doi.org/10.1111/0022-1082.00265

Loewenstein, George, Scott Rick, and Jonathan D. Cohen. "Neuroeconomics." Annual Review of Psychology 59 (2008): 647–72.
https://doi.org/10.1146/annurev.psych.59.103006.093710

Lucey, Brian M., and Michael Dowling. "The Role of Feelings in Investor Decision-making." Journal of Economic Surveys 19, No. 2 (2005): 211–237.
https://doi.org/10.1111/j.0950-0804.2005.00245.x.

Lux, Thomas. "The Socio-economic Dynamics of Speculative Markets: Interacting Agents, Chaos, and the Fat Tails of Return Distributions." Journal of Economic Behavior and Organization 33, No. 2 (1998): 143-165.
https://doi.org/10.1016/S0167-2681(97)00088-7.

Mackay, Charles. 1841. Extraordinary Popular Delusions and the Madness of Crowds. London: R. Bentley.

Madrigal, Vicente. "Non-fundamental Speculation." The Journal of Finance 51, No. 2 (1996): 553-578.
https://doi.org/10.1111/j.1540-6261.1996.tb02694.x.

Marco, Pilar Nogués, and Camila Vam Malle-Sabouret. “East India Bonds, 1718-1763: Early Exotic Derivatives and London Market Efficiency.” European Review of Economic History 11, No. 3 (2007): 367–94. https://doi.org/10.1017/S1361491607002055.

Mathiopoulos, Haris. 1994. Investor’s Small Manual: Wandering through the Sanctuary of the Greek Stock Exchange. Athens: Estia Publications.

Maenhout, Pascal J. “Robust Portfolio Rules and Asset Pricing.” The Review of Financial Studies, 17, No. 4 (2004): 951–983. https://doi.org/10.1093/rfs/hhh003.

Mehra, Rajnish, and Edward C. Prescott. “The Equity Premium: A Puzzle.” Journal of Monetary Economics 15, No. 2 (1985):145−161. https://doi.org/10.1016/0304-3932(85)90061-3.

Menkhoff, Lukas, and Marina Nikiforow. “Professionals’ Endorsement of Behavioral Finance: Does it Impact their Perception of Markets and Themselves?” Journal of Economic Behavior and Organization 71, No. 2 (2009): 318-329. https://doi.org/10.1016/j.jebo.2009.04.004.

Merkle, Christoph. “Emotion and Finance-An Interdisciplinary Approach to the Impact of Emotions on Financial Decision Making.” SSRN Electronic Journal (February 2007). http://doi.org/10.2139/ssrn.1097131.

Merton, Robert C. “A Simple Model of Capital Market Equilibrium with Incomplete Information.” The Journal of Finance 42, No. 3 (1987): 483-510. https://doi.org/10.1111/j.1540-6261.1987.tb04565.x.

Michael, Robert. 2006. Holy Hatred: Christianity, Antisemitism, and the Holocaust. New York: Palgrave Macmillan.

Mosselaar, Jan Sytze. 2018. A Concise Financial History of Europe. Rotterdam: Robeco Global.

Murphy, Antoin E. 1997. John Law. Economic Theorist and Policy-Maker. New York: Oxford University Press.

Nekrasov, Alexander, Siew Hong Teoh, and Shijia Wu. “Limited Attention and Financial Decision Making.” In Handbook of Financial Decision Making, edited by Gilles Hilary and David McLean, 17-35. (London: Edward Elgar Publishing Limited, 2023).

Neuhierl, Andreas, Otto Randl, and Christoph Reschenhofer, and Josef Zechner. “Timing the Factor Zoo.” SSRN Electronic Journal (December 8, 2023). https://dx.doi.org/10.2139/ssrn.4376898.

Nogueira, de Vasconcelos Antonio. “The Portuguese Jews and Modern Capitalism. Trading, Insurance, Banking, Business, and Economic Thought in Amsterdam from earlier 16th to the first decades of 20th centuries." Presentation at the XXII Encontro APHES conference, Aveiro, Portugal (15/11/2002).

Nogueira, de Vasconcelos Antonio. "The Portuguese Jews in the Business Network of Glückel of Hameln (1646-1724)." Presentation at the 1st Congress of Sephardic Identity and Memory, Bragança, Portugal (15-18/6/2017).

Nusteling, Hurbert P.H. "The Jews in the Republic of the United Provinces: Origin, Numbers and Dispersion." In Dutch Jewry: Its History and Secular Culture (1500-2000), edited by Jonathan Israel and Reinier Salverda, 43-62. (Leiden: Brill, 2002).

Obadiah 1:20, In King James Bible. (Glasgow: Collins, 2016).

Odean, Terrance. "Do Investors Trade Too Much?" American Economic Review 89, No. 5 (1999): 1279–1298. https://doi.org/10.1257/aer.89.5.1279.

Payzan-Le Nestour, Elize. "Neurofinance". In Handbook of Financial Decision Making, edited by David McLean and Gilles Hillary, 91-109. (London: Edward Elgar Publishing, 2023).

Peng, Lin, and Wei Xiong. "Investor Attention, Overconfidence and Category Learning." Journal of Financial Economics 80, No. 3 (2006): 563-602. https://doi.org/10.1016/j.jfineco.2005.05.003

Pérez, Joseph. 2007. History of a Tragedy: The Expulsion of the Jews from Spain. Champaign: University of Illinois Press.

Peterson, Richard L. "Neurofinance." In Investor behavior: The psychology of financial planning and investing, edited by H. Kent Baker and Victor Ricciardi, 381-401. (New Jersey: John Wiley & Sons, Inc, 2014).

Petram, Lodewijk. 2014. The World's First Stock Exchange. New York: Columbia Business School Publishing.

Pierdzioch, Christian. "Feedback Trading and Predictability of Stock Returns in Germany, 1880-1913." Working Paper No. 1213, Kiel Institute for World Economics (May 2004). https://hdl.handle.net/10419/17763.

Plastun, Alex, Xolani Sibande, Rangan Gupta, and Mark E. Wohar. "Rise and Fall of Calendar Anomalies over a Century." The North American Journal of Economics and Finance 49 (2019): 181-205. https://doi.org/10.1016/j.najef.2019.04.011.

Pleßner, Marco. "The Disposition Effect: A Survey." Management Review Quarterly 67 (2017): 1–30. https://doi.org/10.1007/s11301-017-0122-6

Putniņš, Tālis J. "Market Manipulation: A Survey." Journal of Economic Surveys 26, No. 5 (2012): 952–967.

https://doi.org/10.1111/j.1467-6419.2011.00692.x.

Putniņš, Tālis J. "An Overview of Market Manipulation." In Corruption and Fraud in Financial Markets (1st ed.), edited by Carol Alexander and Douglas Cumming, 13–44. (New Jersey: John Wiley & Sons Inc, 2020).

Risen, Jane L. "Believing what we do not Believe: Acquiescence to Superstitious Beliefs and Other Powerful Intuitions." Psychological Review 123, No. 2 (2016): 182–207. https://doi.org/10.1037/rev0000017.

Roitman, Jessica. "Marriage, Migration, and Money: The Santa Companhia de dotar orphãs e donzelas pobres in the Portuguese Sephardic Diaspora." Portuguese Studies 13, No. 1 (2005): 347-367.

Ross, Stephen A. "Information and Volatility: The No-Arbitrage Martingale Approach to Timing and Resolution Irrelevancy." The Journal of Finance 44, No. 1 (1989): 1–17. https://doi.org/10.2307/2328272.

Roth, Norman. 1994. Jews, Visigoths and Muslims in medieval Spain: cooperation and conflict. Leiden: Brill.

Rutterford, Janette, Dimitris P. Sotiropoulos, and Carry Van Lieshout. "Individual Investors and Local Bias in the UK, 1870-1935." Economic History Review 70, No. 4 (2017): 1291-1320. https://doi.org/10.1111/ehr.12482.

Samuelson, William, and Richard Zeckhauser. "Status Quo Bias in Decision Making." Journal of Risk and Uncertainty 1, No. 1 (1988): 7-59. https://doi.org/10.1007/BF00055564.

Sapra, Steven and Paul J. Zak. "Neurofinance: Bridging Psychology, Neurology, and Investor Behavior." SSRN Electronic Journal (December 1, 2008). https://dx.doi.org/10.2139/ssrn.1323051.

Sargent, Thomas J. 1993. Bounded Rationality in Macroeconomics. Oxford University Press.

Savage, Leonard J. 1964. The Foundations of Statistics. New York: Wiley.

Schöffer, I. "The Jews in The Netherlands: The Position Of A Minority Through Three Centuries." Studia Rosenthaliana 15, No. 1 (1981): 85–100. http://www.jstor.org/stable/41481887.

Scholes, Myron S. "The Market for Securities: Substitution Versus Price Pressure and the Effects of Information on Share Prices." The Journal of Business 45, No. 2 (1972): 179–211. https://doi.org/10.1086/295444.

Schorsch, Jonathan. "Blacks, Jews and the Racial Imagination in the Writings of Sephardim in the Long Seventeenth Century." Jewish History 19, No. 1 (2005): 109–35. https://doi.org/10.1007/s10835-005-4360-0.

Selden, George C. 1919. Psychology of the Stock Market. Magazine of Wall Street: New York.

Shi, Leilei, Liyan Han, Yiwen Wang, Ding Chen, Yan Piao, and Chengling Gou. "Market Crowd Trading Conditioning and its Measurement." SSRN Electronic Journal (November 5, 2011). https://dx.doi.org/10.2139/ssrn.1661515.

Shiller, Robert J. "Do Stock Prices Move Too Much to Be Justified by Subsequent Changes in Dividends?" The American Economic Review 71, No. 3 (1981): 421–36. http://www.jstor.org/stable/1802789.

Shleifer, Andrei, and Robert W. Vishny. "The Limits of Arbitrage." The Journal of Finance 52, No. 1 (1997): 35–55. https://doi.org/10.2307/2329555.

Sicherman, Nachum, George Loewenstein, Duane J. Seppi, and Stephen P. Utkus. "Financial Attention." The Review of Financial Studies 29, No. 4 (2016): 863–97. https://doi.org/10.1093/rfs/hhv073.

Simon, Herbert A. "Theories of Decision-Making in Economics and Behavioral Science." The American Economic Review 49, No. 3 (1959): 253–83. https://doi.org/10.1007/978-1-349-00210-8_1.

So, Eric C., and Sean Wang. "News-driven Return Reversals: Liquidity Provision ahead of Earnings Announcements." Journal of Financial Economics 114, No. 1 (2014): 20-35. https://doi.org/10.1016/j.jfineco.2014.06.009.

Stambaugh, Robert F., Jianfeng Yu, and Yu Yuan. "Arbitrage Asymmetry and the Idiosyncratic Volatility Puzzle." The Journal of Finance 70, No. 5 (2015): 1903–48. https://doi.org/10.1111/jofi.12286.

Stein, Edward. 1996. Without Good Reason–The Rationality Debate in Philosophy and Cognitive Science. Oxford: Clarendon Press.

Stillman, Norman. "Aspects of Jewish Life in Islamic Spain." In Aspects of Jewish Culture in the Middle Ages, edited by Paul E. Szarmach, 51-84. (Albany: State University of New York Press, 1979).

Strahilevitz, Michal Ann, Terrance Odean, and Brad M. Barber. "Once Burned, Twice Shy: How Naive Learning, Counterfactuals, and Regret

Affect the Repurchase of Stocks Previously Sold." Journal of Marketing Research 48 (2011): 102–120. https://doi.org/10.1509/jmkr.48.SPL.S102.

Stringham, Edward. "The Extralegal Development of Securities Trading in Seventeenth-century Amsterdam." The Quarterly Review of Economics and Finance 43, No. 2 (2003): 321-344. https://doi.org/10.1016/S1062-9769(02)00153-9.

Sul, Hong Kee, Alan R. Dennis, and Lingyao (Ivy) Yuan. "Trading on Twitter: Using Social Media Sentiment to Predict Stock Returns." Decision Sciences 48, No. 3 (2017): 454-488. https://doi.org/10.1111/deci.12229.

Sutcliffe, Adam. "Review of *Sephardic Amsterdam and the Myths of Jewish Modernity*," by Steven Nadler, David Liss, Willi Goetschel, Rebecca Goldstein, Manfred Walther, Elhanan Yakira, Heidi M. Ravven, et al. The Jewish Quarterly Review 97, No. 3 (2007): 417–37. http://www.jstor.org/stable/25470215.

Swetschinski, Daniel M. "Kinship and Commerce: The Foundations of Portuguese Jewish Life in Seventeenth-Century Holland." Studia Rosenthaliana 15, No. 1 (1981): 52–74. http://www.jstor.org/stable/41481885.

Szpiro, George G. 2011. Pricing the Future. Finance, Physics, and the 300-year journey to the Black-Scholes Equation. New York: Basic Books Group.

Taffler, Richard. "Emotional Finance: Investment and the Unconscious." The European Journal of Finance 24, No. 7-8 (2018): 630-653. https://doi.org/10.1080/1351847X.2017.1369445.

Takatsuki, Yasuo, and Taro Hisamatsu. "The Role of Information in the Rice Exchange: YAMAGATA Bantō's *Great Knowledge* (1806)." The European Journal of the History of Economic Thought 30, No. 3 (2023): 395-409. https://doi.org/10.1080/09672567.2023.2190598

Teh, Lillyn L., and Werner F.M. DeBondt. "Herding Behavior and Stock Returns: An Exploratory Investigation." Swiss Journal of Economics and Statistics 133, No. 2/2 (1997): 293–324.

Tetlock, Paul C. "Giving Content to Investor Sentiment: The Role of Media in the Stock Market." The Journal of Finance 62, No. 3 (2007): 1139–68. https://doi.org/10.1111/j.1540-6261.2007.01232.x.

Thaler, Richard. H., and Cass R. Sunstein. 2009. Nudge. Improving Decisions about Health, Wealth, and Happiness. London: Penguin Books.

Torisson, Fredrik. "A Conditioned Exchange." The Human, Conditioned 13, No. 2(25; 2019): 47-68. https://doi.org/10.7480/footprint.13.2.3407.

Tripathi, Janhavi S., and Erick W. Rengifo. "The Impact of Fractional Trading on Risk Aversion for Non-professional Investors." Finance Research Letters 52 (2023): 103547. https://doi.org/10.1016/j.frl.2022.103547

Trivellato, Francesca. "Jews and the Early Modern Economy." In The Cambridge History of Judaism, edited by Jonathan Karp and Adam Sutcliffe, 139–67. (Cambridge: Cambridge University Press, 2017).

Tversky, Amos, and Daniel Kahneman. "Judgment under Uncertainty: Heuristics and Biases." Science 185, No. 4157 (1974): 1124−1131. https://doi.org/10.1126/science.185.4157.1124.

Tversky, Amos, and Daniel Kahneman. "Rational Choice and the Framing of Decisions." The Journal of Business 59, No. 4 (1986): 251–278. https://doi.org/10.1007/978-3-642-74919-3_4.

Tversky, Amos, and Daniel Kahneman. "Advances in Prospect Theory: Cumulative Representation of Uncertainty." Journal of Risk and Uncertainty 5, No. 4 (1992): 297-323. https://doi.org/10.1007/BF00122574.

Ülkü, Numan, and Olena Onishchenko. "Institutional Overcrowding Everyday." Journal of Behavioral Finance 24, No. 1 (2023): 1-21. https://doi.org/10.1080/15427560.2021.1892678.

Van Bommel, Jos. "Rumors." The Journal of Finance 58, No. 4 (2003): 1499-1520. https://doi.org/10.1111/1540-6261.00575.

van der Lem, Anton. 2019. Revolt in the Netherlands: The Eighty Years War, 1568–1648. London: Reaktion Books.

Vaihekoski Mika. "Helsinki Stock Exchange: Trading and Listed Securities, 1912-1981." Financial History Review 29, No. 3 (2022): 326-341. https://doi.org/10.1017/S0968565022000208

von Neumann, John., and Oscar Morgenstern. 1944. Theory of Games and Economic Behavior. New Jersey: Princeton University Press.

Wang, Zijun. "The High Volume Return Premium and Economic Fundamentals." Journal of Financial Economics 140, No. 1 (2021): 325-345. https://doi.org/10.1016/j.jfineco.2020.10.006.

Waud, Roger N. "Public Interpretation of Federal Reserve Discount Rate Changes: Evidence on the 'Announcement Effect.'" Econometrica 38, No. 2 (1970): 231–50.

https://doi.org/10.2307/1913006.

Woo, Kai-Yin, Chulin Mai, Michael McAleer, and Wing-Keung Wong. "Review on Efficiency and Anomalies in Stock Markets." Economies 8, No. 1 (2020): 20.

Zak, Paul J. "Neuroeconomics." Philosophical Transactions of the Royal Society B 359, No. 1451 (2004): 1737-1748. https://doi.org/10.1098/rstb.2004.1544.